THE
BAKING
BIBLE

Good Housekeeping

THE BAKING BIBLE

THE ULTIMATE BAKER'S COMPANION

COLLINS & BROWN

First published in Great Britain in 2011
by Collins & Brown
10 Southcombe Street
London W14 0RA

An imprint of Anova Books Company Ltd.

This edition published in 2011 for WHSmith

The Good Housekeeping website is
www.allaboutyou.com/goodhousekeeping

ISBN 978-1-84340-668-6

A catalogue record for this book is available from the British Library.

Reproduction by Dot Gradations Ltd, UK
Printed and bound by Everbest Printing Co Ltd, China

This book can be ordered direct from the publisher at
www.anovabooks.com

NOTES

- Both metric and imperial measures are given for the recipes.
  Follow either set of measures, not a mixture of both, as they
  are not interchangeable.

- All spoon measures are level.
  1 tsp = 5ml spoon; 1 tbsp = 15ml spoon.

- Ovens and grills must be preheated to the specified
  temperature.

- Use sea salt and freshly ground black pepper unless otherwise
  suggested.

- Fresh herbs should be used unless dried herbs are specified in
  a recipe.

- Medium eggs should be used except where otherwise
  specified. Free-range eggs are recommended.

DIETARY GUIDELINES

- Note that some recipes contain raw or lightly cooked eggs. The
  young, elderly, pregnant women and anyone with an immune-
  deficiency disease should avoid these, because of the slight risk
  of salmonella.

- Note that some recipes contain alcohol. Check the ingredients
  list before serving to children.

CONTENTS

FOREWORD

Baking has always had a welcome place in people's hearts. It promises not only a house filled with tantalising aromas, but also the satisfaction of feeding those you love with irresistible sweet treats – not to mention yourself! With the rise of the patisserie outlet and excellent shop-bought cakes, there's always the threat of 'the easy way out' but, good though these shop-bought cakes and bakes may be, they are not homemade.

For me, this self-madeness shows you care and it's hard not to feel a nibbling of pride when you're surrounded by munching sounds of delight. On the flip side, if a little mishap does occur and, say, your scones have not risen to the heavens, you'll know they still taste good.

In my experience, baking is what hooks most people into enjoying their kitchen – and with good reason, it's fun! Even if you haven't started at a tender age, stamping out dinosaur biscuits, there's always time to learn and to be rewarded with the huge sense of satisfaction of seeing something cooling on a wire rack.

Baking involves a delicate – scientific, even – balance, where a small change in an ingredient can have a large effect on the finished result. It's hard to 'wing it' when baking. But fear not, baking is very simple if you follow a good recipe closely – and Good Housekeeping recipes are not only excellent, but have also been triple-tested in our dedicated kitchens, so you are sure to succeed.

I hope you enjoy this book – it's filled with sweet promise.

Meike

Meike Beck
Cookery Editor
Good Housekeeping

CAKES

THE PERFECT VICTORIA SPONGE

● ● ● ● ● ● ● ● ● ● ● ● ● ● ● ● ● ● ●

CUTS INTO 10 SLICES

Preparation: 20 minutes

Cooking time: about 25 minutes, plus cooling

175g (6oz) unsalted butter at room temperature, plus extra
   to grease
175g (6oz) golden caster sugar
3 medium eggs
175g (6oz) self-raising flour, sifted
3–4 tbsp jam
a little icing sugar to dust

PER SLICE

445 cals; 21g fat (of which 11g saturates); 30g carbohydrate; 0.8g salt

1 Grease two 18cm (7 inch) sandwich tins and base-line with
   greaseproof paper. Preheat the oven to 190°C (170°C fan
   oven) mark 5.
2 Put the butter and caster sugar into a large bowl and, using a
   hand-held electric whisk, beat together until pale and fluffy.
   Add the eggs, one at a time, beating well after each addition
   and adding a spoonful of flour to the mixture if it looks as if it's
   about to curdle. Using a large metal spoon, fold in the
   remaining flour.
3 Divide the mixture evenly between the prepared tins and level
   the surface with a palette knife. Bake in the centre of the oven
   for 20–25 minutes until the cakes are well risen and spring
   back when lightly pressed in the centre. Loosen the edges with
   a palette knife and leave in the tins for 5 minutes.
4 Turn out, remove the lining paper and leave to cool on a wire
   rack. Sandwich the two cakes together with jam and dust icing
   sugar over the top. Slice and serve.

TO STORE

Store in an airtight container. It will keep for up to three days.
If stored in the fridge it will keep for up to one week.

CHOCOLATE VICTORIA SANDWICH

● ● ● ● ● ● ● ● ● ● ● ● ● ● ● ● ● ● ●

CUTS INTO 8 SLICES

Preparation: 20 minutes
Cooking time: 20 minutes, plus cooling

175g (6oz) unsalted butter at room temperature, plus extra to grease
3 tbsp cocoa powder
175g (6oz) golden caster sugar
3 medium eggs, beaten
160g (5½oz) self-raising flour, sifted
golden caster sugar to dredge

CHOCOLATE BUTTERCREAM

1 tbsp cocoa powder
75g (3oz) unsalted butter, softened
175g (6oz) icing sugar, sifted
a few drops of vanilla extract
1–2 tbsp milk or water

PER SLICE

520 cals; 30g fat (of which 19g saturates); 62g carbohydrate; 1g salt

1 Preheat the oven to 190°C (170°C fan oven) mark 5. Grease two 18cm (7 inch) sandwich tins and base-line with baking parchment. Blend the cocoa powder with 3 tbsp hot water to make a smooth paste, then leave to cool.
2 Using a freestanding mixer or hand-held electric whisk, cream the butter and sugar together until pale and fluffy. Add the cooled cocoa mixture and beat until evenly blended.
3 Add the beaten eggs, a little at a time, beating well after each addition. Using a metal spoon or large spatula, fold in half the flour, then carefully fold in the rest. Divide the mixture evenly between the tins and level the surface.
4 Bake both cakes on the middle shelf of the oven for about 20 minutes until well risen, springy to the touch and beginning to shrink away from the sides of the tins. Cool in the tins for 5 minutes, then turn out on to a wire rack and leave to cool completely.
5 To make the chocolate buttercream, blend the cocoa powder with 3 tbsp boiling water and set aside to cool. Put the butter into a bowl and beat with a wooden spoon until light and fluffy. Gradually stir in the icing sugar. Add the blended cocoa, vanilla extract and milk or water and beat well until light and smooth.
6 When the cakes are cool, sandwich them together with the chocolate buttercream and sprinkle the top with caster sugar.

TO STORE

Store in an airtight container in a cool place. It will keep well for up to one week.

WHISKED SPONGE

● ●

CUTS INTO 6–8 SLICES

Preparation: 25 minutes
Cooking time: 20–25 minutes, plus cooling

butter to grease
90g (3oz) plain flour, plus extra to dust
3 large eggs
125g (4oz) golden caster sugar

TO ASSEMBLE
3–4 tbsp strawberry, raspberry or apricot jam
125ml (4fl oz) whipping cream, whipped (optional)
caster or icing sugar to dust

PER SLICE (WITHOUT CREAM)
215–160 cals; 4–3g fat (of which 0.9–0.7g saturates); 30–24g carbohydrate; 0.1g salt

1 Preheat the oven to 190°C (170°C fan oven) mark 5. Grease and base-line two 18cm (7 inch) sandwich tins and dust the sides with a little flour or with a mixture of flour and caster sugar.
2 Put the eggs and sugar into a large heatproof bowl and, using a hand-held electric whisk, whisk until well blended. Put the bowl over a pan of hot water and whisk until pale and creamy and thick enough to leave a trail on the surface when the whisk is lifted. Remove the bowl from the pan and whisk until cool and thick.
3 Sift half the flour over the mixture and, using a large metal spoon or plastic-bladed spatula, fold it in very lightly. Sift in the remaining flour and fold in gently until evenly incorporated.
4 Pour the mixture into the prepared tins, tilting the tins to spread the mixture evenly. Bake in the middle of the oven for 20–25 minutes until well risen and springy to the touch when lightly pressed in the centre. Turn out on to a wire rack and leave to cool.
5 Sandwich the cakes together with jam, and cream, if you like. Dust with caster or icing sugar to serve.

NOTE
This classic fatless sponge does not keep well and is best eaten on the day it is made.

VARIATION
Chocolate whisked sponge:
Replace 1½ tbsp of the flour with 1½ tbsp cocoa powder. Sandwich the cake layers together with vanilla or chocolate buttercream (see page 321). Dust with icing sugar.

SWISS ROLL

●●●●●●●●●●●●●●●●●●●●●●●●●●●●●●●●●●●●●

CUTS INTO 8 SLICES

Preparation: 25 minutes
Cooking time: 10–12 minutes, plus cooling

butter to grease
125g (4oz) golden caster sugar, plus extra to dust
125g (4oz) plain flour, plus extra to dust
3 large eggs

TO ASSEMBLE
caster sugar to sprinkle
125g (4oz) jam, warmed

PER SLICE
200 cals; 3g fat (of which 0.7g saturates); 41g carbohydrate; 0.9g salt

1 Grease and line a 33 x 23cm (13 x 9 inch) Swiss roll tin (see page 306). Grease the paper, then dust with caster sugar and flour. Preheat the oven to 200°C (180°C fan oven) mark 6.

2 Put the eggs and sugar into a large heatproof bowl and, using a hand-held electric whisk, whisk until well blended. Put the bowl over a pan of hot water and whisk until the mixture is pale and creamy and thick enough to leave a trail on the surface when the whisk is lifted. Remove the bowl from the pan and whisk until cool and thick.

3 Sift half the flour over the mixture and fold it in very lightly, using a large metal spoon or spatula. Sift in the remaining flour and gently fold in until evenly incorporated. Carefully fold in 1 tbsp hot water.

4 Pour into the prepared tin and tilt the tin backwards and forwards to spread the mixture evenly. Bake for 10–12 minutes until pale golden, risen and springy to the touch.

5 Meanwhile, put a sheet of greaseproof paper on a damp teatowel. Dredge the paper with caster sugar.

6 Quickly turn out the cake on to the paper and remove the lining paper. Trim off the crusty edges and spread the cake with jam.

7 Using the greaseproof paper to help, roll up the cake from a short side. Make the first turn firmly so that the cake will roll evenly and have a good shape when finished, but roll more lightly after this turn. Put seam-side down on a wire rack and sprinkle with sugar to serve.

VARIATION
Chocolate Swiss roll:
Replace 1 tbsp flour with cocoa powder. Turn out and trim the sponge as above, then cover with a sheet of greaseproof paper and roll with the paper inside. When cold, unroll and remove the paper. Spread with whipped cream or buttercream (see page 314) and re-roll. Dust with icing sugar.

CARROT CAKE

● ● ● ● ● ● ● ● ● ● ● ● ● ● ● ● ● ● ● ●

CUTS INTO 12 SLICES

Preparation: 15 minutes
Cooking time: 40 minutes, plus cooling

250ml (9fl oz) sunflower oil, plus extra to grease
225g (8oz) light muscovado sugar
3 large eggs
225g (8oz) self-raising flour
large pinch of salt
½ tsp each ground mixed spice, ground nutmeg and ground
   cinnamon
250g (9oz) carrots, peeled and coarsely grated

FROSTING

50g (2oz) butter, preferably unsalted, at room temperature
225g pack cream cheese
25g (1oz) golden icing sugar
½ tsp vanilla extract
8 pecan halves, roughly chopped

PER SLICE

383 cals; 32g fat (of which 10g saturates); 24g carbohydrate; 0.3g salt

1. Preheat the oven to 180°C (160°C fan oven) mark 4. Grease two 18cm (7 inch) sandwich tins and base-line with greaseproof paper.
2. Using a hand-held electric whisk, whisk the oil and muscovado sugar together to combine, then whisk in the eggs, one at a time.
3. Sift the flour, salt and spices together over the mixture, then gently fold in, using a large metal spoon. Tip the carrots into the bowl and fold in.
4. Divide the cake mixture between the prepared tins and bake for 30–40 minutes until golden and a skewer inserted into the centre comes out clean. Remove from the oven and leave in the tins for 10 minutes, then turn out on to a wire rack and leave to cool completely.
5. To make the frosting, beat the butter and cream cheese together in a bowl until light and fluffy. Sift in the icing sugar, add the vanilla extract and beat well until smooth. Spread one-third of the frosting over one cake and sandwich together with the other cake. Spread the remaining frosting on top and sprinkle with the pecans.

TO STORE

Store in an airtight container. Eat within two days. Alternatively, the cake will keep for up to one week in an airtight container if it is stored before the frosting is applied.

ALMOND AND APRICOT CAKE

● ● ● ● ● ● ● ● ● ● ● ● ● ● ● ● ● ● ●

CUTS INTO 12 SLICES

Preparation: 15 minutes
Cooking time: 15 minutes, plus cooling

175g (6oz) unsalted butter, softened, plus extra to grease
125g (4oz) caster sugar
4 medium eggs
175g (6oz) self-raising flour
75g (3oz) ground almonds
finely grated zest and juice of 1 lemon

ICING AND FILLING
250g tub mascarpone cheese
40g (1½oz) icing sugar, plus extra to dust
4 tbsp apricot compote

PER SLICE
325 cals; 21g fat (of which 11g saturates); 30g carbohydrate; 0.3g salt

1 Preheat the oven to 200°C (180°C fan oven) mark 6. Grease two 18cm (7 inch) round sandwich tins and line with greaseproof paper.

2 Beat the butter and caster sugar together until fluffy. Then beat in the eggs, one at a time, until combined. Using a metal spoon, gently fold in the flour, ground almonds, lemon zest and juice and stir until smooth.

3 Divide the mixture between the tins, level the surface and bake for 15 minutes or until golden and a skewer inserted into the centre comes out clean. Cool in the tins for 5 minutes, then turn out on to a wire rack and leave to cool completely.

4 For the icing, beat the mascarpone and icing sugar together in a bowl. Spread over one of the cakes. Spoon the apricot compote evenly over the cheese mixture and put the other cake on top. Dust with icing sugar to serve.

TO STORE
Store in an airtight container in a cool place. It will keep for up to two days.

MADEIRA CAKE

CUTS INTO 12 SLICES

Preparation: 20 minutes

Cooking time: about 50 minutes, plus cooling

175g (6oz) butter, softened, plus extra to grease
125g (4oz) plain flour
125g (4oz) self-raising flour
175g (6oz) golden caster sugar
1 tsp vanilla extract
3 large eggs, beaten
1–2 tbsp milk (optional)
2–3 thin slices citron peel

PER SLICE

260 cals; 14g fat (of which 8g saturates); 31g carbohydrate; 0.4g salt

1 Preheat the oven to 180°C (160°C fan oven) mark 4. Grease and line a deep 18cm (7 inch) round cake tin. Sift the plain and self-raising flours together.

2 Cream the butter and sugar together in a bowl until pale and fluffy, then beat in the vanilla extract. Add the eggs, a little at a time, beating well after each addition.

3 Using a metal spoon, fold in the sifted flours, adding a little milk if necessary to give a dropping consistency.

4 Spoon the mixture into the prepared tin and level the surface. Bake for 20 minutes. Lay the citron peel on the cake and bake for a further 30 minutes or until a skewer inserted into the centre comes out clean. Turn out on to a wire rack and leave to cool. This cake can be made up to one week in advance (store in an airtight tin) or frozen for up to one month.

VARIATION

Add the grated zest of 1 lemon at stage 2. Add the juice of the lemon instead of the milk at stage 3.

Quantities and sizes for Madeira cakes

To make a Madeira sponge cake follow the method above, choosing your tin size and corresponding ingredient amounts from the chart below:

Square tin size	Round tin size	Makes	Baking time	Ingredients
12.5cm (5 inch)	15cm (6 inch)	8–10 slices	1–1¼ hours	125g (4oz) each of softened unsalted butter and golden caster sugar; 2 medium eggs; 125g (4oz) sifted self-raising flour; 50g (2oz) sifted plain flour; grated zest and juice of ½ lemon
15cm (6 inch)	18cm (7 inch)	20 slices	1¼ hours	225g (8oz) each of softened unsalted butter and golden caster sugar; 4 medium eggs; 225g (8oz) sifted self-raising flour; 100g (3½oz) sifted plain flour; grated zest and juice of 1 lemon
23cm (9 inch)	25.5cm (10 inch)	28 slices	1 hour 20–30 minutes	350g (12oz) each of softened unsalted butter and golden caster sugar; 6 medium eggs; 350g (12oz) sifted self-raising flour; 175g (6oz) sifted plain flour; grated zest and juice of 1½ lemons

RICH FRUIT CAKE

CUTS INTO 16 SLICES

Preparation: 30 minutes
Cooking time: 2½ hours, plus cooling

175g (6oz) unsalted butter, cubed, plus extra to grease
1kg (2¼lb) mixed dried fruit
100g (3½oz) ready-to-eat dried prunes, roughly chopped
50g (2oz) ready-to-eat dried figs, roughly chopped
100g (3½oz) dried cranberries
2 balls preserved stem ginger in syrup, grated and syrup reserved
grated zest and juice of 1 orange
175ml (6fl oz) brandy
2 splashes Angostura bitters
175g (6oz) dark muscovado sugar
200g (7oz) self-raising flour
½ tsp ground cinnamon
½ tsp freshly grated nutmeg
½ tsp ground cloves
4 medium eggs, beaten

PER SLICE

277 cals; 11g fat (of which 6g saturates); 38g carbohydrate; 0.2g salt

1   Preheat the oven to 150°C (130°C fan oven) mark 2. Grease a
    20.5cm (8 inch) round, deep cake tin and line base and sides
    with greaseproof paper.
2   Put all the dried fruit into a very large pan and add the ginger,
    1 tbsp reserved ginger syrup, the orange zest and juice, brandy
    and Angostura bitters. Bring to the boil, then simmer for
    5 minutes. Add the butter and sugar and heat gently to melt.
    Stir occasionally until the sugar dissolves. Take the pan off the
    heat and leave to cool for a couple of minutes.
3   Add the flour, spices and beaten eggs and mix well. Pour the
    mixture into the prepared tin and level the surface. Wrap the
    outside of the tin in brown paper and secure with string to
    protect the cake during cooking. Bake for 2–2½ hours – cover
    with greaseproof paper after about 1½ hours – until the cake
    is firm to the touch and a skewer inserted into the centre
    comes out clean.
4   Cool in the tin for 2–3 hours, then remove from the tin,
    leaving the greaseproof paper on, transfer to a wire rack and
    leave to cool completely. Wrap the cake in a layer of clingfilm,
    then in foil.

TO STORE

Store in an airtight container. It will keep for up to three months.
If you like, after the cake has matured for two weeks, prick it all
over with a metal skewer and sprinkle with 1 tbsp brandy. Leave
to soak in, then rewrap and store as before.

Quantities and sizes for Rich Fruit Cakes

To make a formal cake for a birthday, wedding or anniversary, the following chart will show you the amount of ingredients required to fill the chosen cake tin or tins, whether round or square.

NOTE

When baking large cakes, 25.5cm (10 inch) and upwards, it is advisable to reduce the oven heat to 130°C (110°C fan) mark 1 after two-thirds of the cooking time. The amounts of Almond Paste quoted in this chart will give a thin covering. The quantities of Royal Icing should be enough for two coats. If using ready-to-roll fondant icing, use the quantities suggested for Royal Icing as a rough guide.

Size	Square tin size	Round tin size	Cooking time (approx.)	Weight when cooked	Ingredients	Almond Paste	Royal Icing
Size 1	12.5cm (5 inch)	15cm (6 inch)	2½–3 hours	1.1kg (2½lb)	225g (8oz) currants, 125g (4oz) each sultanas and raisins, 50g (2oz) glacé cherries, 25g (1oz) each mixed peel and flaked almonds, a little lemon zest, 175g (6oz) plain flour, 4 tsp each mixed spice and cinnamon, 150g (5oz) each softened butter and soft brown sugar; 2½ medium eggs, beaten, 1 tbsp brandy	350g (12oz)	450g (1lb)
Size 2	15cm (6 inch)	18cm (7 inch)	3 hours	1.6kg (3½lb)	350g (12oz) currants, 125g (4oz) each sultanas and raisins, 75g (3oz) glacé cherries, 50g (2oz) each mixed peel and flaked almonds, a little lemon zest, 200g (7oz) plain flour, ½ tsp each mixed spice and cinnamon, 175g (6oz) each softened butter and soft brown sugar; 3 medium eggs, beaten, 1 tbsp brandy	450g (1lb)	550g (1¼lb)
Size 3	20.5cm (8 inch)	23cm (9 inch)	4 hours	2.7kg (6lb)	625g (1lb 6oz) currants, 225g (8oz) each sultanas and raisins, 175g (6oz) glacé cherries, 125g (4oz) each mixed peel and flaked almonds, zest of ¼ lemon, 400g (14oz) plain flour, 1 tsp each cinnamon and mixed spice, 350g (12oz) each softened butter and soft brown sugar, 6 medium eggs, beaten, 2 tbsp brandy	800g (1¾lb)	900g (2lb)
Size 4	23cm (9 inch)	25.5cm (10 inch)	6 hours	4kg (9lb)	800g (1¾lb) currants, 375g (13oz) each sultanas and raisins, 250g (9oz) glacé cherries, 150g (5oz) each mixed peel and flaked almonds, zest of ¼–½ lemon, 600g (1lb 5oz) plain flour, 1 tsp each mixed spice and cinnamon, 500g (1lb 2oz) each softened butter and soft brown sugar, 9 medium eggs, beaten, 2–3 tbsp brandy	900g (2lb)	1kg (2¼lb)
Size 5	28cm (11 inch)	30.5cm (12 inch)	8 hours	6.7kg (14¾lb)	1.5kg (3lb 2oz) currants, 525g (1lb 3oz) each sultanas and raisins, 350g (12oz) glacé cherries, 250g (9oz) each mixed peel and flaked almonds, zest of ½ lemon, 825g (1lb 13oz) plain flour, 2½ tsp each mixed spice and cinnamon, 800g (1¾lb) each softened butter and soft brown sugar, 14 medium eggs, beaten, 4 tbsp brandy	1.1kg (2½lb)	1.4kg (3lb)
Size 6	30.5cm (12 inch)	33cm (13 inch)	8½ hours	7.7kg (17lb)	1.7kg (3lb 12oz) currants, 625g (1lb 6oz) each sultanas and raisins, 425g (15oz) glacé cherries, 275g (10oz) each mixed peel and flaked almonds, zest of 1 lemon, 1kg (2¼lb) plain flour, 2½ tsp each mixed spice and cinnamon, 950g (2lb 2oz) each softened butter and soft brown sugar, 17 medium eggs, beaten, 6 tbsp brandy	1.4kg (3lb)	1.6kg (3½lb)

BANANA AND BUTTERSCOTCH LOAF

● ● ● ● ● ● ● ● ● ● ● ● ● ● ● ● ● ● ● ●

CUTS INTO 15 SLICES

Preparation: 20 minutes
Cooking time: 1 hour, plus cooling

butter to grease
175g (6oz) plain flour, sifted
2 tsp baking powder
½ tsp bicarbonate of soda
½ tsp salt
175g (6oz) light muscovado sugar
2 large eggs
3 medium-size ripe bananas, peeled and mashed
150g carton natural yogurt
150g bar butterscotch chocolate, roughly chopped
100g (3½oz) pecan nuts, chopped
1–2 tbsp demerara sugar

PER SLICE

221 cals; 9g fat (of which 2g saturates); 34g carbohydrate; 0.2g salt

1 Preheat the oven to 170°C (150°C fan oven) mark 3. Grease a 1.4kg (3lb) loaf tin and line with greaseproof paper.
2 Put the flour, baking powder, bicarbonate of soda and salt into a large bowl and mix together.
3 In a separate bowl, beat the muscovado sugar and eggs together with a hand-held electric whisk until pale and fluffy. Carefully stir in the bananas, yogurt, chocolate and 50g (2oz) pecan nuts, followed by the flour mixture.
4 Spoon the mixture into the prepared tin and level the surface. Sprinkle with the remaining chopped pecan nuts and the demerara sugar. Bake for 1 hour or until a skewer inserted into the centre comes out clean. Leave to cool in the tin on a wire rack, then turn out and slice.

TO STORE

Store in an airtight container. It will keep for up to two days.

VARIATION

If you can't find butterscotch chocolate, use a bar of plain dark chocolate instead.

STICKY LEMON POLENTA CAKE

● ●

CUTS INTO 12 SLICES

Preparation: 10 minutes

Cooking time: 1 hour, plus cooling

50g (2oz) unsalted butter, softened, plus extra to grease
3 lemons
250g (9oz) golden caster sugar
250g (9oz) instant polenta
1 tsp baking powder
2 large eggs
50ml (2fl oz) semi-skimmed milk
2 tbsp natural yogurt
2 tbsp poppy seeds

PER SLICE

220 cals; 7g fat (of which 3g saturates); 37g carbohydrate; 0.1g salt

1 Preheat the oven to 180°C (160°C fan oven) mark 4. Lightly grease a 900g (2lb) loaf tin and base-line with greaseproof paper.

2 Grate the zest of 1 lemon and put into a food processor with the butter, 200g (7oz) sugar, the polenta, baking powder, eggs, milk, yogurt and poppy seeds, then whiz until smooth. Spoon the mixture into the prepared tin and level the surface. Bake for 55 minutes–1 hour until a skewer inserted into the centre comes out clean. Leave to cool in the tin for 10 minutes.

3 Next, make a syrup. Squeeze the juice from the zested lemon plus 1 more lemon. Thinly slice the third lemon. Put the lemon juice into a pan with the remaining sugar and 150ml (¼ pint) water. Add the lemon slices, bring to the boil and bubble for about 10 minutes until syrupy. Take the pan off the heat and leave to cool for 5 minutes. Remove the lemon slices from the syrup and set aside.

4 Slide a knife around the edge of the cake and turn out on to a serving plate. Pierce the cake in several places with a skewer, spoon the syrup over it and decorate with the lemon slices.

TO STORE

Wrap in clingfilm and store in an airtight container. It will keep for up to three days.

LEMON DRIZZLE LOAF

CUTS INTO 8–10 SLICES

Preparation: 20 minutes
Cooking time: about 50 minutes, plus cooling

175g (6oz) unsalted butter, softened, plus extra to grease
175g (6oz) caster sugar
4 medium eggs, lightly beaten
3 lemons
125g (4oz) self-raising flour
50g (2oz) ground almonds
75g (3oz) sugar cubes

PER SLICE

424 cals; 25g fat (of which 13g saturates); 46g carbohydrate; 0.6g salt

1 Preheat the oven to 180°C (160°C fan oven) mark 4. Grease a 900g (2lb) loaf tin and line with parchment paper.
2 In a large bowl, beat together the butter and caster sugar with a hand-held electric whisk until pale and fluffy, about 5 minutes. Gradually beat in the eggs, followed by the finely grated zest of 2 of the lemons and the juice of ½ a lemon.
3 Fold the flour and ground almonds into the butter mixture, then spoon into the prepared tin and bake for 40–50 minutes until a skewer inserted into the centre comes out clean. Cool in the tin for 10 minutes, then turn out on to a wire rack and leave to cool until warm.
4 Meanwhile, put the sugar cubes into a small bowl with the juice of 1½ lemons and the pared zest of 1 lemon (you should have 1 un-juiced lemon left over). Soak for 5 minutes, then use the back of a spoon to roughly crush the cubes. Spoon over the warm cake and leave to cool completely before serving in slices.

TO STORE
Store in an airtight container. It will keep for up to four days.

SPICED PECAN, APPLE AND CRANBERRY CAKE

CUTS INTO 8 SLICES

Preparation: 20 minutes
Cooking time: about 1 hour

175g (6oz) unsalted butter, softened, plus extra to grease
150g (5oz) caster sugar
3 medium eggs
1 tsp vanilla extract
150g (5oz) plain flour
1 tsp baking powder
2 tbsp milk
½ tsp ground cinnamon
3 Braeburn apples, peeled, cored and cut into 1cm (½ inch) cubes
50g (2oz) fresh cranberries, defrosted if frozen
75g (3oz) pecan nuts, roughly chopped
2–3 tbsp apricot jam

PER SLICE
436 cals; 28g fat (of which 13g saturates); 44g carbohydrate; 0.5g salt

1 Preheat the oven to 180°C (160°C fan oven) mark 4. Grease a 20.5cm (8 inch)
   springform cake tin and line with baking parchment.
2 Using a freestanding mixer or hand-held electric whisk, beat 150g (5oz) butter with
   the sugar, eggs, vanilla extract, flour, baking powder and milk until pale and fluffy –
   about 5 minutes. Spoon into the prepared tin and level the surface. Bake for
   10 minutes.
3 Meanwhile, heat the remaining butter in a large frying pan until foaming. Stir in the
   cinnamon and apples and cook for 3 minutes until almost tender. Take off the heat
   and stir in the cranberries and pecan nuts.
4 Carefully take the part-baked cake out of the oven and sprinkle the apple mixture
   over the surface. Return to the oven and bake for a further 40–50 minutes until
   a skewer inserted into the centre comes out clean.
5 Leave the cake to cool in the tin for 5 minutes, then remove from the tin and peel off
   the paper. Transfer to a serving plate. Gently warm the jam in a small pan to loosen,
   then brush over the top of the cake. Serve the cake warm or at room temperature.

TO STORE
Store in an airtight container. It will keep for up to two days.

RASPBERRY AND PEACH CAKE

CUTS INTO 8 SLICES

Preparation: 15 minutes
Cooking time: 1–1¼ hours, plus cooling

200g (7oz) unsalted butter, melted, plus extra to grease
250g (9oz) self-raising flour, sifted
100g (3½oz) golden caster sugar
4 medium eggs, beaten
125g (4oz) raspberries
2 large, almost-ripe peaches or nectarines, halved, stoned and sliced
4 tbsp apricot jam
juice of ½ lemon

PER SLICE

405 cals; 24g fat (of which 14g saturates); 44g carbohydrate; 0.8g salt

1 Preheat the oven to 190°C (170°C fan oven) mark 5. Grease a 20.5cm (8 inch) springform cake tin and base-line with baking parchment.
2 Put the flour and sugar into a large bowl. Make a well in the centre and add the melted butter and the eggs. Mix well.
3 Spread half the mixture over the bottom of the cake tin and add half the raspberries and sliced peaches or nectarines. Spoon on the remaining cake mixture, smooth over, then add the remaining raspberries and peaches or nectarines, pressing them down into the mixture slightly.
4 Bake for 1–1¼ hours until risen and golden and a skewer inserted into the centre comes out clean. Remove from the oven and leave in the tin to cool for 10 minutes.
5 Warm the jam and the lemon juice together in a small pan and brush over the cake to glaze. Serve warm or at room temperature.

TO STORE

Store in an airtight container. It will keep for up to one week.

FRUITY TEACAKE

CUTS INTO 12 SLICES

Preparation: 20 minutes, plus soaking
Cooking time: 1 hour, plus cooling

150ml (¼ pint) hot black tea, made with 2 Earl Grey tea bags
200g (7oz) sultanas
75g (3oz) ready-to-eat dried figs, roughly chopped
75g (3oz) ready-to-eat dried prunes, roughly chopped
a little vegetable oil
125g (4oz) dark muscovado sugar
2 medium eggs, beaten
225g (8oz) gluten-free flour
2 tsp wheat-free baking powder
2 tsp ground mixed spice
butter to serve (optional)

PER SLICE

185 cals; 1g fat (of which trace saturates); 42g carbohydrate; 0.1g salt

1 Pour the tea into a bowl and add all the dried fruit. Leave to
   soak for 30 minutes.
2 Preheat the oven to 190°C (170°C fan oven) mark 5. Oil a
   900g (2lb) loaf tin and base-line with greaseproof paper.
3 Beat the sugar and eggs together in a large bowl until pale and
   slightly thickened. Add the flour, baking powder, mixed spice
   and soaked dried fruit and tea, then mix together well. Spoon
   the mixture into the prepared tin and level the surface.
4 Bake on the middle shelf of the oven for 45 minutes–1 hour.
   Leave to cool in the tin.
5 Serve sliced, with a little butter if you like.

TO STORE
Wrap in clingfilm and store in an airtight container. It will keep for
up to five days.

GINGER AND FRUIT TEABREAD

CUTS INTO 12 SLICES

Preparation: 15 minutes, plus soaking
Cooking time: 1 hour, plus cooling

125g (4oz) each dried apricots, apples and pitted prunes, chopped
300ml (½ pint) strong fruit tea
a little butter to grease
25g (1oz) preserved stem ginger in syrup, chopped
225g (8oz) wholemeal flour
2 tsp baking powder
125g (4oz) dark muscovado sugar
1 medium egg, beaten

PER SLICE

145 cals; 1g fat (of which trace saturates); 33g carbohydrate; 0g salt

1 Put the dried fruit into a large bowl, add the tea and leave to soak for 2 hours.
2 Preheat the oven to 180°C (160°C fan oven) mark 4. Grease a 900g (2lb) loaf tin and base-line with baking parchment.
3 Add the remaining ingredients to the soaked fruit and mix thoroughly. Spoon into the prepared tin and brush with 2 tbsp cold water. Bake for 1 hour or until a skewer inserted into the centre comes out clean.
4 Cool in the tin for 10–15 minutes, then turn out on to a wire rack and leave to cool completely.

TO STORE
Wrap in clingfilm and store in an airtight container. It will keep for up to three days.

STICKY GINGERBREAD

BREAD MACHINE RECIPE

CUTS INTO 10 SLICES

Preparation: 15 minutes
Cooking time: 1 hour 10 minutes, plus cooling

125g (4oz) unsalted butter, plus extra to grease
125g (4oz) light muscovado sugar
75g (3oz) black treacle
200g (7oz) golden syrup
250g (9oz) plain flour
2 tsp ground mixed spice
65g (2½oz) preserved stem ginger, finely chopped
2 large eggs
100ml (3½fl oz) milk
1 tsp bicarbonate of soda
extra treacle or golden syrup to glaze (optional)

PER SLICE

341 cals; 12g fat (of which 7g saturates); 58g carbohydrate; 0.7g salt

1 Put the butter, sugar, treacle and golden syrup into a saucepan and heat gently until the butter has melted. Leave to cool for 5 minutes. Grease the bread maker bucket and line with baking parchment, if specified in the manual.

2 Sift the flour and mixed spice together into a bowl. Add the syrup mixture, chopped ginger, eggs and milk and stir well until combined.

3 In a cup, mix the bicarbonate of soda with 2 tbsp hot water, then add to the bowl. Stir the mixture well and pour into the bread maker bucket.

4 Fit the bucket into the bread maker and set to the cake or bake only programme. Select 1 hour 10 minutes on the timer and choose a light crust. Press start.

5 To check whether the cake is done, pierce the centre with a skewer; it should come out fairly clean. If necessary, re-set the timer for a little longer.

6 Remove the bucket from the machine, leave the cake in it for 5 minutes, then turn out on to a wire rack. Brush the top of the cake with the treacle or syrup to glaze, if you like, and leave to cool.

TO STORE

Wrap and store in an airtight container. It will keep for up to one week.

ROCK BUNS

• •

MAKES 12

Preparation: 5 minutes
Cooking time: 20 minutes, plus cooling

125g (4oz) butter or margarine, plus extra to grease
225g (8oz) plain flour
pinch of salt
2 tsp baking powder
75g (3oz) demerara sugar
75g (3oz) mixed dried fruit
zest of ½ lemon
1 medium egg
milk

PER BUN

192 calories; 9g fat (of which 6g saturates); 26g carbohydrate; 0.5g salt

1 Preheat the oven to 200°C (180°C fan oven) mark 6. Lightly grease two baking sheets.
2 Sift together the flour, salt and baking powder. Rub in the butter until the mixture resembles fine breadcrumbs. Add the sugar, fruit and lemon zest and mix together thoroughly.
3 Using a fork, mix to a moist but stiff dough with the beaten egg and a little milk.
4 Using two forks, shape into really rocky heaps on the baking sheets. Bake for about 20 minutes until golden brown. Transfer to a wire rack and leave to cool. Rock buns are best eaten on the day they are made.

NOTE
Use a food processor to whiz the flour and butter together, if you prefer.

MADELEINES

MAKES 24

Preparation: 20 minutes, plus chilling

Cooking time: 10–12 minutes, plus cooling

125g (4oz) unsalted butter, melted and cooled until tepid
125g (4oz) plain flour, plus extra to dust
4 medium eggs
125g (4oz) golden caster sugar
finely grated zest of 1 lemon
1 tsp baking powder
pinch of salt
icing sugar to dust

PER CAKE

90 cals; 5g fat (of which 2g saturates); 10g carbohydrate; 0.2g salt

1 Brush two Madeleine trays with a little of the melted butter. Leave to set, then dust with flour, shaking out any excess.
2 Using a hand-held electric whisk, beat the eggs, sugar and lemon zest together in a bowl, until the mixture is pale, creamy and thick enough to leave a trail when the whisk is lifted.
3 Sift in half the flour, together with the baking powder and salt. Carefully pour in half the melted butter around the edge of the bowl and gently fold in until evenly incorporated. Repeat with the remaining flour and butter. Cover and chill the mixture in the fridge for 45 minutes. Preheat the oven to 220°C (200°C fan oven) mark 7.
4 Two-thirds fill the Madeleine moulds with the mixture and bake for 10–12 minutes until well risen and golden. Ease out of the tins, transfer to a wire rack and leave to cool. Serve dusted with icing sugar.

NOTES
- Resting the sponge mixture before baking gives the Madeleines their characteristic dense texture.
- If you have only one Madeleine tray, then bake in two batches.

CHOCOLATE WHOOPIE PIES

● ●

MAKES 18–20

Preparation: 30 minutes
Cooking time: 12 minutes

1 large egg
150g (5oz) caster sugar
75g (3oz) butter, melted
150g (5oz) crème fraîche
1 tsp vanilla extract
1½–2 tbsp milk
200g (7oz) plain flour
75g (3oz) cocoa powder
½ tsp bicarbonate soda

FILLING
115g (3¾oz) unsalted butter, softened
200g (7oz) icing sugar, sifted
1 tsp vanilla extract
milk (optional)

PER PIE
365 cals; 14g fat (of which 8g saturates); 59g carbohydrate; 0.3g salt

1 Preheat the oven to 180°C (160°C fan oven) mark 4. Line two large baking sheets
   with baking parchment.
2 Whisk the egg and caster sugar together until thick and light in colour. Beat in the
   melted butter, crème fraîche, vanilla extract and milk.
3 Sift together the flour, cocoa powder and bicarbonate of soda. Beat into the egg
   mixture until smooth – it will make a very thick mixture but should be pipable. Add a
   drop more milk if necessary.
4 Fill a piping bag fitted with a large nozzle with the mixture and pipe walnut-sized balls
   on to the baking sheets, spacing well apart. Bake for 10–12 minutes until golden and
   risen. Cool on the baking sheet for 1–2 minutes until firm, then transfer to a wire rack
   and leave to cool completely.
5 To make the filling, cream together the butter and icing sugar until fluffy. Beat in the
   vanilla extract. Beat in a little milk, if necessary, to make the icing a spreadable
   consistency. Sandwich the whoopie halves together with the buttercream.

BLACK FOREST ROULADE

• • • • • • • • • • • • • • • • • • • •

CUTS INTO 10 SLICES

Preparation: 35 minutes
Cooking time: 20 minutes, plus cooling and chilling

4 large eggs, separated
125g (4oz) golden caster sugar, plus extra to dust
125g (4oz) plain chocolate (at least 70% cocoa solids), broken into pieces, melted (see tips) and left to cool a little
cocoa powder and icing sugar to dust
chocolate curls (see tips) to decorate (optional)

FILLING

140ml (4½fl oz) whipping cream
1 tsp icing sugar
75g (3oz) Greek-style yogurt
2 x 425g cans morello cherries, drained, pitted and halved

PER SLICE

248 cals; 12g fat (of which 7g saturates); 33g carbohydrate; 0.1g salt

1 Preheat the oven to 180°C (160°C fan oven) mark 4. Line a 33 x 23cm (13 x 9 inch) Swiss roll tin with baking parchment.
2 Whisk the egg yolks with the sugar in a large bowl until thick and creamy. Whisk in the melted chocolate. Whisk the egg whites in a clean, grease-free bowl until stiff peaks form. Fold into the chocolate mixture. Pour into the prepared tin, level the surface and bake for 20 minutes or until firm to the touch. Leave to cool in the tin for 10–15 minutes.
3 Put a sheet of baking parchment on the worksurface and dust with caster sugar. Carefully turn out the roulade on to the parchment and peel off the lining parchment. Cover with a damp cloth and leave to cool for 30 minutes.
4 To make the filling, lightly whip the cream with the icing sugar, then fold in the yogurt. Spread over the cold roulade and scatter the cherries on top. Using the baking parchment to help, roll up the roulade from one of the narrow ends. Chill for 30 minutes. Dust with cocoa powder and icing sugar, decorate with chocolate curls, if you like, and serve sliced.

TIPS
Melted chocolate:
Break chocolate into pieces and place in a heatproof bowl. Set over a pan of gently simmering water, making sure the base of the bowl doesn't touch the water. Heat very gently until the chocolate starts to melt, then stir regularly until completely melted.

Chocolate curls:
Spread melted chocolate out in a thin layer on a marble slab or clean worksurface. Leave to firm up. Using a sharp, flat-ended blade (such as a pastry scraper or a very stiff spatula), scrape through the chocolate at a 45-degree angle. The size of the curls will be determined by the width of the blade.

DECADENT CHOCOLATE CAKE

● ● ● ● ● ● ● ● ● ● ● ● ● ● ● ● ● ● ●

CUTS INTO 12 SLICES

Preparation: 30 minutes

Cooking time: 1½ hours, plus cooling and setting

225g (8oz) unsalted butter, softened, plus extra to grease

300g (11oz) plain chocolate, broken into pieces

225g (8oz) golden caster sugar

225g (8oz) ground almonds

8 large eggs, separated

125g (4oz) fresh brown breadcrumbs

4 tbsp apricot jam (optional)

cream to serve (optional)

GANACHE

175g (6oz) plain chocolate, broken into pieces

75g (3oz) butter, softened

4 tbsp double cream

PER SLICE

687 cals; 49g fat (of which 23g saturates); 54g carbohydrate; 0.7g salt

1 Preheat the oven to 180°C (160°C fan oven) mark 4. Grease a 23cm (9 inch) springform cake tin and line with greaseproof paper.

2 Melt the chocolate in a heatproof bowl set over a pan of gently simmering water, making sure the base of the bowl doesn't touch the water. Remove the bowl from the pan.

3 Put the butter and sugar into a large bowl and beat until light and creamy. Add the almonds, egg yolks and breadcrumbs. Beat well until thoroughly mixed. Slowly add the chocolate and carefully stir it in. Do not over-mix, as the chocolate may seize up and become unworkable.

4 Put the egg whites into a clean, grease-free bowl and whisk until stiff peaks form. Add half the whites to the chocolate mixture and, using a large metal spoon, fold in lightly. Carefully fold in the remainder. Pour into the prepared tin and level the surface.

5 Bake for 1 hour 20 minutes or until the cake is firm to the touch and a skewer inserted into the centre comes out clean. Cool in the tin for 5 minutes, then transfer to a wire rack and leave for 2–3 hours to cool completely.

6 Put the jam, if using, into a pan and melt over a low heat. Brush jam over the top and sides of the cake.

7 Melt the chocolate, butter and cream in a heatproof bowl set over a pan of gently simmering water, making sure the base of the bowl doesn't touch the water. Stir just once until smooth. Either raise the cake off the worksurface on the upturned tin or put it (still on the rack) on a tray to catch the drips. Pour the ganache into the centre and tip the cake to let it run down the sides evenly, or spread it with a palette knife. Leave to set then serve with cream, if you like.

BLACK FOREST GATEAU

SERVES 12

Preparation: 30 minutes
Cooking time: about 50 minutes, plus cooling

125g (4oz) unsalted butter, melted
200g (7oz) plain flour
50g (2oz) cornflour
50g (2oz) cocoa powder, plus extra to dust
2 tsp espresso instant coffee powder
1 tsp baking powder
4 large eggs, separated
300g (11oz) golden caster sugar
2 × 300g jars morello cherries in syrup
2 tbsp Kirsch
200ml (7fl oz) double cream
2 tbsp icing sugar, sifted
fresh cherries and chocolate curls (see page 40) to decorate

PER SERVING

440 cals; 22g fat (of which 12g saturates); 59g carbohydrate; 0.8g salt

1 Preheat the oven to 180°C (160°C fan oven) mark 4. Brush a little of the melted butter over the base and sides of a 20.5cm (8 inch) round × 9cm (3½ inch) deep cake tin. Line the base and sides with baking parchment.

2 Sift the flour, cornflour, cocoa powder, coffee powder and baking powder together three times – this helps to add air and makes sure the ingredients are well mixed.

3 Put the egg yolks, caster sugar and 100ml (3½fl oz) cold water into a freestanding mixer and whisk for 8 minutes until the mixture leaves a trail for 3 seconds when the whisk is lifted.

4 Add the rest of the melted butter, pouring it around the edge of the bowl so that the mixture doesn't lose any air, then quickly fold it in, followed by the sifted flour mixture in two batches.

5 In another bowl, whisk the egg whites until stiff peaks form, then fold a spoonful into the cake mixture to loosen. Carefully fold in the rest of the egg whites, making sure there are no white blobs left. Pour into the prepared tin and bake in the oven for 45–50 minutes until a skewer inserted into the centre comes out clean. Leave in the tin for 10 minutes, then turn out on to a wire rack to cool completely.

6 When the cake is cold, trim the top to make a flat surface. Turn the cake over so that the top becomes the base. Using a long serrated bread knife, carefully cut into three horizontally. Drain the cherries, reserving 250ml (9fl oz) of the syrup. Put the syrup into a pan and simmer to reduce by half. Stir in the Kirsch. Brush the hot syrup on to each layer of the cake – including the top – using up all the liquid.

7 Lightly whip the cream with the icing sugar. Spread one-third over the bottom layer of cake and cover with half the cherries. Top with the next cake layer and repeat with another third of the cream and the remaining cherries. Top with the final cake layer and spread the remaining cream over. Decorate with fresh cherries, chocolate curls and a dusting of cocoa powder.

NOTE
Make the gateau up to two hours ahead to allow the flavours to mingle and the syrup to moisten the cake.

CARDAMOM AND MANGO CAKE

● ●

CUTS INTO 10 SLICES

Preparation: 45 minutes
Cooking time: 25–30 minutes, plus cooling and chilling

50g (2oz) unsalted butter, plus extra to grease
4 green cardamom pods, split and seeds removed
a good pinch of saffron strands
4 large eggs
125g (4oz) caster sugar
100g (3½oz) plain flour

FILLING, MANGO SAUCE AND DECORATION
2 large, ripe mangoes
150ml (¼ pint) double cream
150g (5oz) Greek-style yogurt
3 tbsp icing sugar, plus extra to dust
4 tbsp orange juice
orange segments

PER SLICE
274 cals; 16g fat (of which 9g saturates); 31g carbohydrate; 0.2g salt

1 Preheat the oven to 180°C (160°C fan oven) mark 4. Grease two 18cm (7 inch) sandwich tins, or one deep 18cm (7 inch) round cake tin, and base-line with baking parchment.

2 Crush the cardamom seeds to a powder together with the saffron. Put the butter into a pan and heat gently until melted, then remove from the heat and leave to cool for a few minutes until beginning to thicken.

3 Put the eggs and caster sugar into a large heatproof bowl. Using a hand-held electric whisk, whisk until evenly blended. Put the bowl over a pan of hot water and whisk until pale and thick enough to leave a trail on the surface when the whisk is lifted. Remove the bowl from the pan and whisk until cool and thick.

4 Sift the spices and flour together. Using a large metal spoon or plastic spatula, fold half into the whisked mixture. Pour the cooled butter around the edge of the mixture, leaving the sediment behind. Gradually fold it in very lightly, cutting through the mixture until it is all incorporated. Carefully fold in the remaining flour as lightly as possible. Pour into the prepared tins.

5 Bake for 25–30 minutes until well risen and the cakes spring back when lightly pressed. Run a small knife around the cake edge to loosen and leave in the tins for 5 minutes, then turn out on to a wire rack and leave to cool completely.

6 To make the filling, peel the mangoes, then cut one of them into slices. Whip the cream until it holds its shape. Stir in the yogurt with 2 tbsp icing sugar. Sandwich the cakes with the cream mixture and mango slices. Chill for 2–3 hours.

7 To make the mango sauce, put the remaining mango flesh, 1 tbsp icing sugar and the orange juice into a blender and whiz to a purée. Pass the purée through a nylon sieve to remove all the fibres. Cover and chill.

8 Just before serving, decorate the cake with orange segments and dust with icing sugar. Serve with the mango sauce.

BEST-EVER LEMON GATEAU

OVERNIGHT PREPARATION NEEDED

CUTS INTO 8 SLICES

Preparation: 35 minutes
Cooking time: about 20 minutes, plus cooling and chilling

butter to grease
2½ tbsp semolina, plus extra to dust
6 large eggs, separated
150g (5oz) caster sugar
2 large lemons
40g (1½oz) ground almonds
3 tbsp plain flour
3 gelatine leaves
150ml (¼ pint) double cream
icing sugar to dust

PER SLICE

276 cals; 17g fat (of which 7g saturates); 28g carbohydrate; 0.2g salt

1 Preheat the oven to 180°C (160°C fan oven) mark 4. Grease an 8cm (3¼ inch) deep, 20.5cm (8 inch) loose-based round tin. Base-line with baking parchment and dust the sides with semolina.

2 Put 3 egg yolks, 50g (2oz) sugar and the zest of 1 lemon into a bowl and beat for 5 minutes. Fold in the semolina, almonds and flour.

3 Put 3 egg whites into a clean, grease-free bowl and whisk until stiff. Add 25g (1oz) sugar and beat for a few seconds. Fold 1 tbsp into the cake mixture, then fold in the rest. Spoon into the prepared tin and level the surface. Bake for 15–20 minutes. Leave to cool in the tin.

4 Remove the sides of the tin and slide the cake on to a board, leaving the parchment in place. Slice the cake in half horizontally. Regrease and reline the sides of the tin with baking parchment, then put the cake half with the paper attached into the tin, paper side down.

5 Put the gelatine into a bowl and cover with cold water. Leave for 5 minutes. Heat the juice of 1 lemon until simmering. Squeeze the excess water from the gelatine, then whisk into the lemon juice. Leave to cool. Whisk the remaining yolks and sugar with the zest of the other lemon until mousse-like. Fold the gelatine mixture into the sugar and lemon mixture.

6 Put the remaining egg whites into a clean, grease-free bowl and whisk until stiff. Whip the cream until it just holds its shape. Fold the cream into the yolk mix, then fold in the egg whites. Pour into the tin, cover and chill for 2 hours. Put the second cake layer over the mousse, cut-side down. Cover and chill overnight.

7 Turn out the cake and peel off the paper. Dust with icing sugar. Heat a metal skewer in a gas flame and score lines on the top.

CREAMY COFFEE AND PRALINE GATEAU

CUTS INTO 8 SLICES

Preparation: 45 minutes
Cooking time: 25 minutes, plus cooling

50g (2oz) unsalted butter, melted, plus extra to grease
125g (4oz) plain flour, sifted, plus extra to dust
4 large eggs, separated
125g (4oz) caster sugar
1 tbsp coffee granules, dissolved in 2 tsp boiling water

PRALINE
50g (2oz) whole blanched hazelnuts
150g (5oz) caster sugar

FILLING
500g (1lb 2oz) mascarpone cheese
250g (9oz) icing sugar, sifted
2 tbsp coffee granules, dissolved in 1 tbsp boiling water

PER SLICE
548 cals; 21g fat (of which 10g saturates); 83g carbohydrate; 0.2g salt

1 Preheat the oven to 190°C (170°C fan oven) mark 5. Grease two 18cm (7 inch) loose-based sandwich tins. Dust lightly with flour and tip out the excess.
2 Put the egg whites into a clean, grease-free bowl and whisk until soft peaks form. Whisk in 1 egg yolk; repeat with the other 3 yolks. Add the sugar, 1 tbsp at a time, and continue to whisk. The mixture should be thick enough to leave a trail when the whisk is lifted. Using a large metal spoon, fold half the flour into the mixture.
3 Mix the coffee into the melted butter, then pour around the edge of the egg mixture. Add the remaining flour and gradually fold in. Divide the mixture between the prepared tins and bake for 25 minutes or until risen and firm to the touch. Turn out on to a wire rack and leave to cool completely.
4 To make the praline, line a baking sheet with non-stick baking parchment and scatter the nuts on it. Dissolve the sugar in a heavy-based pan over a low heat, shaking the pan once or twice to help it dissolve evenly. Cook until it forms a dark golden-brown caramel. Pour over the nuts and leave to cool.
5 To make the filling, put the mascarpone and icing sugar into a large bowl, add the coffee and mix with a hand-held electric whisk. Slice each cake in half horizontally. Put one cake layer on a plate and spread with a quarter of the filling. Continue layering in this way, finishing with a layer of mascarpone filling.
6 Break the praline into two or three pieces and put into a plastic bag. Using a rolling pin, smash it into smaller pieces. Use to decorate the top of the cake.

GLUTEN-FREE CHOCOLATE CAKE

CUTS INTO 10 SLICES

Preparation: 30 minutes
Cooking time: 45 minutes–1 hour, plus cooling

125g (4oz) unsalted butter, softened, plus extra to grease
200g (7oz) light muscovado sugar
2 large eggs, lightly beaten
125g (4oz) gluten-free plain chocolate, broken into pieces, melted
  (see page 40) and left to cool slightly
100g (3½oz) natural yogurt
a few drops of vanilla extract
200g (7oz) brown rice flour
½ tsp wheat-free baking powder
1 tsp bicarbonate of soda

ICING

150g (5oz) gluten-free plain chocolate, broken into pieces
150ml (¼ pint) double cream
large milk and plain or white chocolate buttons (gluten-free) to
  decorate

PER SLICE

476 cals; 28g fat (of which 16g saturates); 60g carbohydrate; 0.3g salt

1 Preheat the oven to 180°C (160°C fan oven) mark 4. Grease
   a deep 18cm (7 inch) square cake tin and line with
   greaseproof paper.
2 Cream the butter and sugar together until light and fluffy.
   Gradually beat in the eggs, then the melted chocolate, yogurt
   and vanilla extract. Sift the rice flour, baking powder and
   bicarbonate of soda together, then beat into the mixture a little
   at a time. Pour into the prepared tin and bake for 45 minutes–
   1 hour until a skewer inserted into the centre comes out clean.
   Cool in the tin for 10 minutes, then turn out on to a wire rack
   and leave to cool completely.
3 To make the icing, put the chocolate into a heatproof bowl.
   Heat the cream to just below boiling point. Pour on to the
   chocolate and leave for 5 minutes, then beat until the
   chocolate has melted and the mixture is smooth. Cool until
   thickened, then, using a palette knife, spread all over the cake.
   Decorate the top and sides with alternate milk and plain or
   white chocolate buttons to create a polka-dot effect.

TO STORE

Store in an airtight container. It will keep for up to three days.

TOASTED HAZELNUT MERINGUE CAKE

CUTS INTO 8 SLICES

Preparation: 10 minutes
Cooking time: about 30 minutes, plus cooling

oil to grease
175g (6oz) skinned hazelnuts, toasted
3 large egg whites
175g (6oz) golden caster sugar
250g carton mascarpone cheese
285ml (9½fl oz) double cream
3 tbsp Bailey's Irish Cream liqueur, plus extra to serve
140g (4½oz) frozen raspberries
340g jar redcurrant jelly

PER SLICE

598 cals; 38g fat (of which 16g saturates); 57g carbohydrate; 0.1g salt

1 Preheat the oven to 190°C (170°C fan oven) mark 5. Lightly oil two 18cm (7 inch) sandwich tins and base-line with baking parchment. Whiz the hazelnuts in a food processor until finely chopped.

2 Put the egg whites into a clean, grease-free bowl and whisk until stiff peaks form. Whisk in the sugar, a spoonful at a time. Using a metal spoon, fold in half the nuts. Divide the mixture between the tins and spread evenly. Bake in the middle of the oven for about 30 minutes, then leave to cool in the tins for 30 minutes.

3 To make the filling, put the mascarpone cheese into a bowl. Beat in the cream and liqueur until smooth. Put the raspberries and redcurrant jelly into a pan and heat gently until the jelly has melted. Sieve, then cool.

4 Use a palette knife to loosen the edges of the meringues, then turn out on to a wire rack. Peel off the baking parchment and discard. Put a large sheet of baking parchment on a board and sit one meringue on top, flat-side down. Spread one-third of the mascarpone mixture over the meringue, then drizzle with raspberry purée. Top with the other meringue, then cover the whole cake with the rest of the mascarpone mixture. Sprinkle with the remaining hazelnuts. Carefully put the cake on to a serving plate and drizzle with more liqueur, if you like.

FREEZING TIP

Freezing the meringue makes it slightly softer but no less tasty. Complete the recipe to the end of step 4, but don't put on a serving plate or drizzle with more liqueur. Using the paper, lift the cake into the freezer, then freeze until solid. Once solid, store in a sturdy container in the freezer for up to one month. To use, thaw overnight in the fridge, then complete the recipe.

EASTER CHOCOLATE FUDGE CAKE

• • • • • • • • • • • • • • • • • • • •

CUTS INTO 12 SLICES

Preparation: 30 minutes
Cooking time: about 50 minutes, plus cooling

175g (6oz) unsalted butter, softened, plus extra to grease
150g (5oz) plain flour
50g (2oz) cocoa powder
1 tsp baking powder
pinch of salt
150g (5oz) light muscovado sugar
3 medium eggs, beaten
250ml (9fl oz) soured cream
1 tsp vanilla extract

ICING AND DECORATION
100g (3½oz) plain chocolate, finely chopped
150g (5oz) unsalted butter, softened
125g (4oz) cream cheese
175g (6oz) icing sugar, sifted
50g (2oz) chocolate curls, lightly crushed (see page 40)
foil-covered chocolate eggs

PER SLICE
590 cals; 42g fat (of which 25g saturates); 50g carbohydrate; 0.7g salt

1 Preheat the oven to 180°C (160°C fan oven) mark 4. Grease a 20.5cm (8 inch) springform tin and line with greaseproof paper. Sift the flour, cocoa powder, baking powder and salt into a large bowl.
2 Using an electric mixer or electric beaters, mix the butter and muscovado sugar in a separate bowl until pale and fluffy – about 5 minutes. Gradually add the beaten eggs, mixing well after each addition. Add a little of the flour mixture if the butter mixture looks like curdling. In one go, add the remaining flour mixture, the soured cream and vanilla extract, then fold everything together gently with a metal spoon. Spoon into the prepared tin and bake for 40–50 minutes until a skewer inserted into centre comes out clean. Cool in the tin.

3 To make the icing, melt the chocolate in a heatproof bowl set over a pan of barely simmering water, making sure the base of the bowl doesn't touch the water. Leave to cool for 15 minutes. In a separate bowl, beat the butter and cream cheese with a wooden spoon until combined. Beat in the icing sugar, then the cooled chocolate. Take care not to over-beat the mixture – it should be fudgey, not stiff.
4 Remove the cake from the tin, cut in half horizontally and use some icing to sandwich the layers together. Transfer to a cake stand, then ice the top and sides, smoothing with a palette knife. Decorate with crushed curls and chocolate eggs.

WHITE CHOCOLATE CAPPUCCINO CAKE

CUTS INTO 10 SLICES

Preparation: 45 minutes

Cooking time: about 50 minutes, plus cooling

300g (11oz) unsalted butter, at room temperature, plus extra
    to grease
250g (9oz) self-raising flour, plus extra to dust
200g (7oz) caster sugar
3 large eggs, at room temperature, beaten
1½ tsp baking powder
50ml (2fl oz) milk
1 tsp vanilla extract
125g (4oz) white chocolate
125ml (4fl oz) double cream
1½–2 tbsp espresso coffee, cooled
75g (3oz) icing sugar, sifted, plus extra to dust
50g (2oz) plain chocolate, grated
40g (1½oz) hazelnuts, roasted and chopped
small roses to decorate

PER SLICE

659 cals; 45g fat (of which 25g saturates); 60g carbohydrate; 0.3g salt

1 Preheat the oven to 180°C (160°C fan oven) mark 4. Grease
   a deep non-stick 20.5cm (8 inch) cake tin and dust with flour.
2 Beat together the caster sugar and 175g (6oz) butter until pale
   and creamy. Gradually add the eggs, beating well after each
   addition. Add 1 tbsp flour if the mix looks like curdling. Fold in
   the remaining flour and the baking powder, followed by the
   milk and vanilla extract. Spoon into the prepared tin and level
   the surface. Bake for 40–50 minutes until a skewer inserted
   into the centre comes out clean. Cool in the tin for 5 minutes,
   then turn out on to a wire rack and leave to cool completely.
3 Cut the cake in half horizontally. Grate 25g (1oz) white
   chocolate, then beat together with the cream and coffee until
   the mixture holds its shape. Use to sandwich the two cake
   halves together.
4 Melt the remaining white chocolate in a bowl set over a pan of
   simmering water (see page 40). Leave to cool for 10 minutes.
   Beat together the remaining butter and the icing sugar until
   pale and creamy. Beat in the cooled white chocolate, then
   spread over the sides and top of the cake.
5 Mix the plain chocolate with the nuts and press around
   the side of the cake. Decorate with small roses dusted with
   icing sugar.

NOTE

For convenience, prepare ahead. Make to the end of step 2 up to
24 hours ahead. Return to the tin when cool and wrap in clingfilm.
Complete the recipe to serve.

RED VELVET CAKE

CUTS INTO 10 SLICES

Preparation: 20 minutes
Cooking time: about 1 hour 10 minutes, plus cooling

200g (7oz) unsalted butter, softened, plus extra to grease
250g (9oz) plain flour
40g (1½oz) cocoa powder
1½ tsp baking powder
225g (8oz) caster sugar
2 large eggs, beaten
250ml (9fl oz) soured cream
1 tbsp white wine vinegar
1 tsp bicarbonate of soda
¼ tsp red food colouring paste

FROSTING
400g (14oz) cream cheese
125g (4oz) unsalted butter, softened
125g (4oz) icing sugar
red sugar sprinkles to decorate (optional)

PER SLICE

724 cals, 53g fat (of which 33g saturates); 58g carbohydrate; 1.4g salt

1 Preheat the oven to 180°C (160°C fan oven) mark 4. Grease a 20.5cm (8 inch) deep
   cake tin and line with parchment paper.
2 Sift the flour, cocoa powder and baking powder into a medium bowl. In a separate large
   bowl, beat together the butter and caster sugar with a hand-held electric whisk until pale
   and fluffy, about 5 minutes. Gradually beat in the eggs, until combined.
3 Alternately beat the flour mixture and the soured cream into the butter bowl until
   completely combined. Beat in the vinegar, bicarbonate of soda and food colouring.
   Spoon the mixture into the tin, level the surface and bake for 1 hour–1 hour 10 minutes
   until a skewer inserted into the centre comes out clean. Cool in the tin for 10 minutes,
   then turn out on to a wire rack and leave to cool completely.
4 To make the frosting, put the cream cheese and butter into a large bowl and beat
   together until combined. Sift in the icing sugar and mix well. Halve the cooled cake, then
   sandwich back together using half of the icing. Spread the remaining icing over the top
   of the cake, decorate with sugar sprinkles, if you like, and serve in slices.

TO STORE
Store the finished cake in the fridge. It will keep for up to two days. Allow to reach room
temperature before serving.

BRAN AND APPLE MUFFINS

MAKES 10

Preparation: 20 minutes
Cooking time: 30 minutes, plus cooling

250ml (9fl oz) semi-skimmed milk
2 tbsp orange juice
50g (2oz) All Bran
9 ready-to-eat dried prunes
100g (3½oz) light muscovado sugar
2 medium egg whites
1 tbsp golden syrup
150g (5oz) plain flour, sifted
1 tsp baking powder
1 tsp ground cinnamon
1 eating apple, peeled and grated
demerara sugar to sprinkle

PER MUFFIN

137 cals; 1g fat (of which trace saturates); 31g carbohydrate; 0.3g salt

1 Preheat the oven to 190°C (170°C fan oven) mark 5. Line a bun tin or muffin tin with 10 paper muffin cases.
2 Put the milk, orange juice and All Bran into a bowl and stir to mix. Put to one side for 10 minutes.
3 Put the prunes into a food processor or blender with 100ml (3½fl oz) water and whiz for 2–3 minutes to make a purée, then add the muscovado sugar and whiz briefly to mix.
4 Put the egg whites into a clean, grease-free bowl and whisk until soft peaks form. Add the whites to the milk mixture with the syrup, flour, baking powder, cinnamon, grated apple and prune mixture. Fold all the ingredients together gently – don't over-mix. Spoon the mixture equally into the muffin cases.
5 Bake for 30 minutes or until well risen and golden brown. Transfer to a wire rack and leave to cool completely. Sprinkle with demerara sugar just before serving. These are best eaten on the day they are made.

FREEZING TIP
To freeze, complete the recipe, but don't sprinkle with the sugar topping. Once the muffins are cold, pack, seal and freeze. To use, thaw at cool room temperature. Sprinkle with the sugar to serve.

CHOCOLATE CUPCAKES

MAKES 18

Preparation: 15 minutes
Cooking time: 20 minutes, plus cooling and setting

125g (4oz) unsalted butter, softened
125g (4oz) light muscovado sugar
2 medium eggs, beaten
15g (½oz) cocoa powder
100g (3½oz) self-raising flour
100g (3½oz) plain chocolate (at least 70% cocoa solids),
    roughly chopped

TOPPING
150ml (¼ pint) double cream
100g (3½oz) plain chocolate (at least 70% cocoa solids), broken up

PER CUPCAKE
203 cals; 14g fat (of which 8g saturates); 19g carbohydrate; 0.2g salt

1 Preheat the oven to 190°C (170°C fan oven) mark 5. Line a
   12-hole and a 6-hole bun tin or muffin tin with paper muffin
   cases.
2 Beat the butter and sugar together until light and fluffy.
   Gradually beat in the eggs. Sift the cocoa powder with the
   flour and fold into the creamed mixture with the chopped
   chocolate. Divide the mixture among the paper cases and
   lightly flatten the surface with the back of a spoon.
3 Bake for 20 minutes, then transfer to a wire rack and leave to
   cool completely.
4 For the topping, put the cream and chocolate into a heavy-
   based pan over a low heat and heat until melted, then allow
   to cool and thicken slightly. Spoon on to the cooled cakes,
   then stand the cakes upright on the wire rack and leave for
   30 minutes to set.

TO STORE
Store in an airtight container in the fridge. They will keep for
2–3 days.

FREEZING TIP
To freeze, complete the recipe to the end of step 3. Open-
freeze, then wrap and freeze. To use, thaw for about 1 hour,
then complete the recipe.

THE ULTIMATE CARROT CUPCAKES

● ● ● ● ● ● ● ● ● ● ● ● ● ● ● ● ● ●

MAKES 12

Preparation: 30 minutes
Cooking time: 20 minutes, plus cooling

150g (5oz) carrots, peeled
50g (2oz) raisins
175g (6oz) self-raising flour, sifted
½ tsp bicarbonate of soda
150g (5oz) light soft brown sugar
zest of 1 orange
½ tsp ground mixed spice
3 medium eggs
100ml (3½fl oz) sunflower oil
75ml (2½fl oz) buttermilk

TOPPING AND DECORATION
50g (2oz) icing sugar, sifted
250g (9oz) mascarpone cheese
100g (3½oz) quark cheese
juice of ½ orange
red, yellow and green ready-made fondant icing (optional)

PER CUPCAKE
255 cals; 12g fat (of which 4g saturates); 34g carbohydrate; 0.3g salt

1 Preheat the oven to 190°C (170°C fan oven) mark 5. Line a 12-hole muffin tin with paper muffin cases.
2 Coarsely grate the carrots and put into a large bowl. Add the raisins, flour, bicarbonate of soda, brown sugar, orange zest and mixed spice. Put the eggs, oil and buttermilk into a jug and lightly beat together until combined. Pour the egg mixture into the flour and stir with a spatula until just combined. Divide the mixture equally among the paper cases.
3 Bake for 20 minutes or until lightly golden and risen. Cool in the tin for 5 minutes, then transfer to a wire rack and leave to cool completely.
4 For the topping, mix the icing sugar with the mascarpone, quark and orange juice to a smooth icing. Using a small palette knife, spread a little of the icing over each cake. Use the coloured fondant to make small carrots, if you like, and decorate the cakes with them.

TO STORE
Store in an airtight container in the fridge. They will keep for up to two days.

FREEZING TIP
To freeze, complete the recipe to the end of step 3. Open-freeze, then wrap and freeze. To use, thaw for about 1 hour, then complete the recipe.

TRAYBAKES, BISCUITS AND COOKIES

APRICOT AND ALMOND TRAYBAKE

CUTS INTO 18 BARS

Preparation: 20 minutes
Cooking time: 30–40 minutes, plus cooling

250g (9oz) unsalted butter, softened, plus extra to grease
225g (8oz) golden caster sugar
275g (10oz) self-raising flour, sifted
2 tsp baking powder
finely grated zest of 1 orange and 2 tbsp orange juice
75g (3oz) ground almonds
5 medium eggs, lightly beaten
225g (8oz) ready-to-eat dried apricots, roughly chopped
25g (1oz) flaked almonds
icing sugar to dust (optional)

PER BAR

277 cals; 16g fat (of which 8g saturates); 30g carbohydrate; 0.4g salt

1 Preheat the oven to 180°C (160°C fan oven) mark 4. Grease a 33 × 20.5cm (13 × 8 inch) baking tin and base-line with baking parchment.
2 Put the butter, caster sugar, flour, baking powder, orange zest, ground almonds and eggs into the bowl of a large freestanding mixer. Mix on a low setting for 30 seconds, then increase the speed and mix for 1 minute or until thoroughly combined. (Alternatively, mix well, using a wooden spoon.)
3 Remove the bowl from the mixer. Using a large metal spoon, fold in the apricots. Spoon the mixture into the prepared tin, level the surface and sprinkle the flaked almonds over the top.
4 Bake for 30–40 minutes until risen and golden brown and a skewer inserted into the centre comes out clean. Leave to cool in the tin.
5 Cut into 18 bars. Dust with icing sugar, if you like.

TO STORE
Wrap in clingfilm and store in an airtight container. They will keep for up to three days.

QUICK CHOCOLATE SLICES

● ● ● ● ● ● ● ● ● ● ● ● ● ● ● ● ● ●

CUTS INTO 40 SLICES

Preparation: 10 minutes
Cooking time: 2 minutes, plus chilling

225g (8oz) unsalted butter or olive oil spread, plus extra to grease
50g (2oz) cocoa powder, sifted
3 tbsp golden syrup
300g pack digestive biscuits, crushed
400g (14oz) plain chocolate (at least 70% cocoa solids), broken
    into pieces

PER SLICE

137 cals; 9g fat (of which 6g saturates); 13g carbohydrate; 0.3g salt

1　Grease a 25.5 × 16.5cm (10 × 6½ inch) tin. Put the butter or olive oil spread into a heatproof bowl, add the cocoa powder and syrup and melt over a pan of gently simmering water. Mix everything together.

2　Remove from the heat and stir in the biscuits. Mix well until thoroughly coated in chocolate, crushing any large pieces of biscuit. Turn into the prepared tin and leave to cool, then cover and chill for 20 minutes.

3　Melt the chocolate in a heatproof bowl in a 900W microwave oven on full power for 1 minute 40 seconds, stirring twice. (Alternatively, put into a heatproof bowl set over a pan of gently simmering water, making sure the base of the bowl doesn't touch the water.) Stir once more and pour over the chocolate biscuit base, then chill for 20 minutes.

4　Cut in half lengthways. Cut each half into 20 rectangular slices.

TO STORE
Store in an airtight container. They will keep for up to one week.

BLACKBERRY TRAYBAKE

● ●

CUTS INTO 24 SQUARES

Preparation: 20 minutes
Cooking time: about 45 minutes, plus cooling and setting

275g (10oz) unsalted butter, softened, plus extra to grease
275g (10oz) golden caster sugar
400g (14oz) self-raising flour
1½ tsp baking powder
5 medium eggs, beaten
finely grated zest of 1 large orange
1 tbsp vanilla extract
4–5 tbsp milk
250g (9oz) blackberries
40g (1½oz) flaked almonds

ICING

150g (5oz) icing sugar
1 tsp vanilla extract
about 2 tbsp orange juice

PER SQUARE

239 cals; 12g fat (of which 7g saturates); 32g carbohydrate; 0.4g salt

1 Preheat the oven to 190°C (170°C fan oven) mark 5. Grease a shallow 30.5 x 20.5cm
   (12 x 8 inch) baking tin and line with greaseproof paper.
2 Put the butter and caster sugar into a large bowl. Sift in the flour and baking powder,
   then add the eggs, orange zest and juice, vanilla extract and milk and beat together
   until light and fluffy.
3 Using a metal spoon, fold in half the blackberries. Spoon into the prepared tin and dot
   with the remaining blackberries, then the almonds.
4 Bake for 40–45 minutes until springy to the touch. Cool in the tin for 5 minutes, then
   turn out on to a wire rack and leave to cool completely.
5 When the cake is cool, make the icing. Sift the icing sugar into a bowl, then add the
   vanilla extract and orange juice, mixing as you go, until smooth and runny. Drizzle over
   the cake and leave for 30 minutes to set. Cut into 24 squares to serve.

TO STORE

Wrap in clingfilm and store in an airtight container. It will keep for up to four days.

CARROT TRAYBAKE

CUTS INTO 15 SQUARES

Preparation: 30 minutes
Cooking time: 50 minutes–1 hour 5 minutes, plus cooling

100g (3½oz) unsalted butter, chopped, plus extra to grease
140g (4½oz) carrots, peeled and grated
100g (3½oz) sultanas
100g (3½oz) dried dates, chopped
50g (2oz) tenderised coconut
1 tsp ground cinnamon
½ tsp freshly grated nutmeg
330g bottle maple syrup
150ml (¼ pint) apple juice
zest and juice of 2 oranges
225g (8oz) wholemeal self-raising flour, sifted
2 tsp bicarbonate of soda
125g (4oz) walnut pieces

TOPPING

pared zest from ½–1 orange
200g (7oz) cream cheese
200g (7oz) crème fraîche
2 tbsp icing sugar
1 tsp vanilla extract

PER SQUARE

399 cals; 25g fat (of which 13g saturates); 41g carbohydrate; 0.4g salt

1 Preheat the oven to 190°C (170°C fan oven) mark 5. Grease a 23cm (9 inch) square cake tin and line with greaseproof paper.
2 Put the butter, carrots, sultanas, dates, coconut, spices, syrup, apple juice and orange zest and juice into a large pan. Cover and bring to the boil, then cook for 5 minutes. Tip into a bowl and leave to cool.
3 Put the flour, bicarbonate of soda and walnuts into a large bowl and stir together. Add the cooled carrot mixture and stir well. Spoon the mixture into the prepared tin and level the surface.

4 Bake for 45 minutes–1 hour until firm. Cool in the tin for 10 minutes, then turn out on to a wire rack and leave to cool completely.
5 To make the topping, finely slice the orange zest and put to one side. Put the cream cheese, crème fraîche, icing sugar and vanilla extract into a bowl and stir with a spatula. Spread over the cake and top with the zest. Cut into 15 squares to serve.

TO STORE

Store in an airtight container in the fridge. It will keep for up to two weeks.

CHOCOLATE PECAN BARS

● ● ● ● ● ● ● ● ● ● ● ● ● ● ● ● ●

CUTS INTO 25 BARS

Preparation: 15 minutes

Cooking time: 1¼ hours, plus cooling

200g (7oz) unsalted butter, softened, plus extra to grease
125g (4oz) plain flour, sifted
25g (1oz) icing sugar
1 large egg yolk and 2 large eggs
125g (4oz) self-raising flour
1 tsp baking powder
125g (4oz) caster sugar
3–4 drops vanilla extract
150g (5oz) milk chocolate chips
75g (3oz) pecan nuts, chopped
6 tbsp chocolate and hazelnut spread

PER BAR

189 cals; 13g fat (of which 6g saturates); 18g carbohydrate; 0.2g salt

1 Preheat the oven to 200°C (180°C fan oven) mark 6. Grease a 25.5 × 15cm (10 × 6 inch) shallow baking tin and base-line with baking parchment.
2 Put the plain flour and icing sugar into a food processor with 75g (3oz) roughly chopped butter and whiz until crumb-like in texture. (Alternatively, rub the butter into the dry ingredients in a large bowl by hand or using a pastry cutter.) Add the egg yolk and whiz for 10–15 seconds, or add to the bowl with the dry ingredients and stir until the mixture begins to come together. Turn into the tin and press into a thin layer. Bake for 15 minutes or until golden.
3 Meanwhile, put the self-raising flour, baking powder, caster sugar, vanilla extract and the remaining eggs into the food processor with the remaining softened butter and blend for 15 seconds or until smooth (or put the ingredients into a bowl and mix well with a wooden spoon). Remove the blade and fold in the chocolate chips and pecan nuts. Set aside.

4 Spread the chocolate and hazelnut spread over the cooked base and top with the cake mixture. Lower the oven setting to 180°C (160°C fan oven) mark 4 and bake for 45–50 minutes until golden – cover the top of the cake with foil if it appears to be browning too quickly. Cool in the tin for about 10 minutes, then turn out on to a wire rack and leave to cool completely. Cut into 25 pieces.

TO STORE

Store in an airtight container. They will keep for up to two days.

TRADITIONAL FLAPJACKS

CUTS INTO 12 FLAPJACKS

Preparation: 10 minutes
Cooking time: about 20 minutes, plus cooling

200g (7oz) butter, plus extra to grease
150g (5oz) demerara sugar
4 tbsp golden syrup
1 tsp ground cinnamon
finely grated zest of ½–1 orange
400g (14oz) jumbo oats
100g (3½oz) raisins or sultanas

PER FLAPJACK
354 cals; 17g fat (of which 9g saturates);50g carbohydrate; 0.4g salt

1 Preheat the oven to 190°C (170°C fan oven) mark 5. Grease a 20.5cm (8 inch) square baking tin and line with parchment paper.
2 Melt the butter in a large pan and add the sugar, syrup, cinnamon and orange zest. Heat gently until the sugar dissolves.
3 Remove the pan from the heat and stir in the oats and raisins or sultanas. Press the mixture into the tin and bake for 17–20 minutes until lightly golden. Leave to cool before cutting into squares.

TO STORE
Store in an airtight container. They will keep for up to three days.

APPLE CRUMBLE BARS

CUTS INTO 10 BARS

Preparation: 20 minutes, plus chilling

Cooking time: about 45 minutes, plus cooling

200g (7oz) butter
125g (4oz) caster sugar
200g (7oz) plain flour
pinch of salt
3 dessert apples, peeled, cored and diced into 5mm (¼ inch) cubes
1 tsp ground cinnamon
2 tbsp lemon juice
1 tbsp cornflour
4 tbsp raspberry jam

TOPPING

50g (2oz) pecan nuts, roughly chopped
40g (1½oz) gingernut biscuits, crushed
icing sugar to dust

PER BAR

355 cals, 21g fat (of which 11g saturates); 42g carbohydrate; 0.5g salt

1 Whiz 175g (6oz) butter in a food processor with 75g (3oz) caster sugar for 1 minute. Add the flour and salt and whiz until the mixture just comes together. Wrap the dough in clingfilm and chill for 30 minutes.

2 Preheat the oven to 190°C (170°C fan oven) mark 5 and line an 18cm (7 inch) square baking tin with parchment paper. Push the dough evenly into the bottom of the tin, then prick all over with a fork. Bake for 20–25 minutes until lightly golden, then take out of the oven.

3 Meanwhile, put the remaining butter and caster sugar into a pan with the apples and cinnamon and cook over a gentle heat for 5 minutes or until the apples are softening. In a small bowl, mix the lemon juice with the cornflour, then add this mixture to the apples. Continue to cook, stirring constantly, for 2–3 minutes until the sauce has thickened. Set aside.

4 Warm the jam in a small saucepan, then spread over the shortbread. Top with the apple mixture, then sprinkle the pecan nuts and crushed biscuits over the apples. Bake for 10 minutes, then leave to cool completely in the tin before dusting with icing sugar and cutting into 10 bars.

TO STORE

Store in an airtight container. It will keep for up to four days.

NOTE

For convenience, complete the recipe to the end of step 3 up to one day ahead. Transfer the apple mixture to a bowl and store, covered, in the fridge. Store the shortbread in a tin, covered, at room temperature. Complete the recipe to serve.

DOUBLE-CHOCOLATE BROWNIES

● ● ● ● ● ● ● ● ● ● ● ● ● ● ● ● ● ● ●

CUTS INTO 16 BROWNIES

Preparation: 15 minutes
Cooking time: 20–25 minutes, plus cooling

250g (9oz) unsalted butter, plus extra to grease
250g (9oz) plain chocolate (at least 50% cocoa solids), broken
    into pieces
100g (3½oz) white chocolate, broken into pieces
4 medium eggs
175g (6oz) light muscovado sugar
1 tsp vanilla extract
75g (3oz) plain flour, sifted
¼ tsp baking powder
1 tbsp cocoa powder, sifted, plus extra to dust
100g (3½oz) pecan nuts, chopped
pinch of salt
a little icing sugar to dust

PER BROWNIE
352 cals; 25g fat (of which 13g saturates); 29g carbohydrate; 0.3g salt

1   Preheat the oven to 200°C (180°C fan oven) mark 6. Grease a 20.5cm (8 inch) square shallow tin and base-line with baking parchment. Melt the butter and plain chocolate in a heatproof bowl set over a pan of gently simmering water, making sure the base of the bowl doesn't touch the water. Remove the bowl from the pan and put to one side.

2   In a separate bowl, melt the white chocolate over a pan of gently simmering water, making sure the base of the bowl doesn't touch the water. Remove the bowl from the pan and put to one side.

3   Put the eggs into a separate large bowl. Add the muscovado sugar and vanilla extract and whisk until the mixture is pale and thick. Add the flour, baking powder, cocoa powder, nuts and salt to the bowl, then pour in the dark chocolate mixture. Using a large metal spoon, gently fold the ingredients together to make a smooth batter – if you fold too roughly, the chocolate will seize up and become unusable.

4   Pour the brownie mixture into the prepared tin. Spoon dollops of the white chocolate over the top, then swirl a skewer through it several times to create a marbled effect. Bake for 20–25 minutes. The brownie should be fudgy inside and the top should be cracked and crispy. Leave to cool in the tin.

5   Transfer the brownies to a board and cut into 16 individual brownies. To serve, dust with a little icing sugar and cocoa powder, if you like.

NOTE
For convenience, complete the recipe to the end of step 5, then store in an airtight container. It will keep for up to one week. Complete the recipe to serve.

WHITE CHOCOLATE AND NUT BROWNIES

● ● ● ● ● ● ● ● ● ● ● ● ● ● ● ● ● ● ● ●

CUTS INTO 12 BROWNIES

Preparation: 20 minutes
Cooking time: 30–35 minutes, plus cooling

75g (3oz) unsalted butter, plus extra to grease
500g (1lb 2oz) white chocolate, roughly chopped
3 large eggs
175g (6oz) golden caster sugar
175g (6oz) self-raising flour
pinch of salt
175g (6oz) macadamia nuts, roughly chopped
1 tsp vanilla extract

PER BROWNIE
502 cals; 31g fat (of which 13g saturates); 52g carbohydrate; 0.4g salt

1 Preheat the oven to 190°C (170°C fan oven) mark 5. Grease
   a 25.5 x 20.5cm (10 x 8 inch) baking tin and base-line with
   baking parchment.
2 Melt 125g (4oz) white chocolate with the butter in a
   heatproof bowl set over a pan of gently simmering water,
   making sure the base of the bowl doesn't touch the water,
   stirring occasionally. Remove the bowl from the pan and leave
   to cool slightly.
3 Whisk the eggs and sugar together in a large bowl until
   smooth, then gradually beat in the melted chocolate mixture –
   the consistency will become quite firm. Sift the flour and salt
   over the mixture, then fold in with the nuts, the remaining
   chopped chocolate and the vanilla extract. Turn the mixture
   into the prepared tin and level the surface.
4 Bake for 30–35 minutes until risen and golden and the centre
   is just firm to the touch – the mixture will still be soft under
   the crust; it firms up on cooling. Leave to cool in the tin.
5 Turn out and cut into 12 individual brownies.

TO STORE
Store in an airtight container. They will keep for up to one week.

LAMINGTONS

● ● ● ● ● ● ● ● ● ● ● ● ● ● ● ●

CUTS INTO 16 SQUARES

Preparation: 40 minutes
Cooking time: 30 minutes, plus cooling and setting

125g (4oz) unsalted butter, softened, plus extra to grease
125g (4oz) golden caster sugar
2 medium eggs
125g (4oz) self-raising flour, sifted
1 tsp baking powder
2 tsp vanilla extract

COATING
200g (7oz) icing sugar
50g (2oz) cocoa powder
25g (1oz) unsalted butter, cubed
5 tbsp milk
200g (7oz) desiccated coconut

PER SQUARE
273 cals; 17g fat (of which 12g saturates); 29g carbohydrate; 0.4g salt

1 Preheat the oven to 180°C (160°C fan oven) mark 4. Grease a 15cm (6 inch) square cake tin and base-line with baking parchment.
2 Put the butter, caster sugar, eggs, flour, baking powder and vanilla extract into a bowl and beat with a hand-held electric whisk until creamy. Turn the mixture into the prepared tin and level the surface.
3 Bake for about 30 minutes until just firm to the touch and a skewer inserted into the centre comes out clean. Transfer to a wire rack and leave to cool completely. Wrap and store, preferably overnight, so that the cake is easier to slice.
4 To make the topping, sift the icing sugar and cocoa powder into a bowl. Put the butter and milk into a small pan and heat until the butter has just melted. Pour over the icing sugar and stir until smooth, adding 2–3 tbsp water if necessary, so that the icing thickly coats the back of a spoon.

5 Trim the side crusts from the cake and cut into 16 squares. Place a sheet of greaseproof paper under a wire rack to catch the drips. Scatter the coconut on to a large plate. Pierce a piece of cake through the top crust and dip into the icing until coated, turning the cake gently. Transfer to the wire rack. Once you've coated half the pieces, roll them in the coconut and transfer to a plate. Repeat with the remainder and leave to set for a couple of hours before serving.

NOTE
If, towards the end of coating the cakes, the chocolate topping mixture has thickened, carefully stir in a drop of water to thin it down.

CHOCOLATE CHIP OAT COOKIES

● ● ● ● ● ● ● ● ● ● ● ● ● ● ● ● ● ●

MAKES 18

Preparation: 15 minutes

Cooking time: 12–15 minutes, plus cooling

125g (4oz) unsalted butter, softened, plus extra to grease

125g (4oz) golden caster sugar

1 medium egg

1 tsp vanilla extract

125g (4oz) porridge oats

150g (5oz) plain flour

½ tsp baking powder

200g (7oz) plain chocolate (at least 70% cocoa solids), cut into 1cm (½ inch) chunks

PER COOKIE

197 cals; 10g fat (of which 6g saturates); 26g carbohydrate; 0.2g salt

1 Preheat the oven to 180°C (160°C fan oven) mark 4. Lightly grease two baking sheets.

2 Cream the butter and sugar together in a bowl until pale and creamy. Add the egg, vanilla extract and oats. Sift the flour and baking powder together over the mixture and mix until evenly combined. Stir in the chocolate chunks.

3 Put dessertspoonfuls of the mixture on to the prepared baking sheets, spacing them well apart to allow room for spreading. Flatten each one slightly with the back of a fork.

4 Bake for 12–15 minutes or until risen and turning golden, but still quite soft. Leave on the baking sheet for 5 minutes, then transfer to a wire rack and leave to cool completely.

TO STORE

Store in an airtight container. They will keep for up to one week.

FREEZING TIP

To freeze, complete the recipe and allow the cookies to cool. Wrap, seal, label and freeze. To use, thaw the cookies individually, as needed, at room temperature for 1–2 hours.

SULTANA AND PECAN COOKIES

MAKES 20

Preparation: 15 minutes
Cooking time: 12–15 minutes, plus cooling

225g (8oz) unsalted butter, at room temperature, plus extra
   to grease
175g (6oz) light muscovado sugar
2 medium eggs, lightly beaten
225g (8oz) pecan nut halves
300g (11oz) self-raising flour, sifted
¼ tsp baking powder
125g (4oz) sultanas
2 tbsp maple syrup

PER COOKIE
276 cals; 18g fat (of which 7g saturates); 27g carbohydrate; 0.2g salt

1 Preheat the oven to 190°C (170°C fan oven) mark 5. Lightly
   grease four baking sheets.
2 Cream the butter and sugar together until the mixture is pale
   and fluffy. Gradually beat in the eggs until thoroughly combined.
3 Put 20 pecan nut halves to one side, then roughly chop the
   rest and fold into the mixture with the flour, baking powder,
   sultanas and syrup.
4 Roll the mixture into 20 balls and place them, spaced well
   apart, on the prepared baking sheets. Using a dampened
   palette knife, flatten the cookies and top each with a piece of
   pecan nut.
5 Bake for 12–15 minutes until pale golden. Leave on the baking
   sheets for 5 minutes, then transfer to a wire rack and leave to
   cool completely.

TO STORE
Store in an airtight container. They will keep for up to one week.

FREEZING TIP
To freeze, complete the recipe to the end of step 4, then open-
freeze a tray of unbaked cookies. When frozen, pack into bags
or containers. To use, cook from frozen for 18–20 minutes.

FLORENTINES

● ● ● ● ● ● ● ● ● ● ● ● ● ● ● ● ● ● ●

MAKES 18

Preparation: 15 minutes

Cooking time: 16–20 minutes, plus cooling and setting

65g (2½oz) unsalted butter, plus extra to grease
50g (2oz) golden caster sugar
2 tbsp double cream
25g (1oz) sunflower seeds
20g (¾oz) chopped mixed candied peel
20g (¾oz) sultanas
25g (1oz) natural glacé cherries, roughly chopped
40g (1½oz) flaked almonds, lightly crushed
15g (½oz) plain flour
125g (4oz) plain chocolate (at least 70% cocoa solids), broken
   into pieces

PER BISCUIT

115 cals; 8g fat (of which 4g saturates); 11g carbohydrate; 0.1g salt

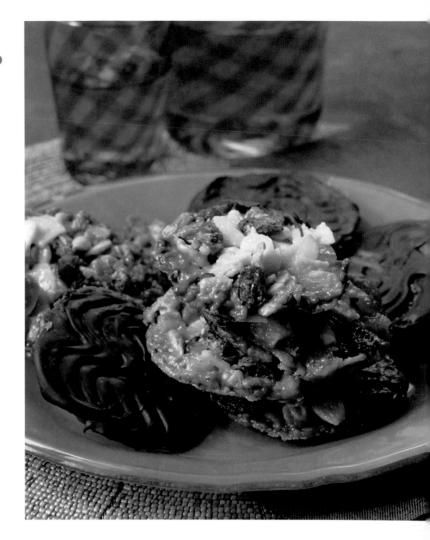

1 Preheat the oven to 180°C (160°C fan oven) mark 4. Lightly grease two large baking sheets.
2 Melt the butter in a small heavy-based pan. Add the sugar and heat gently until dissolved, then bring to the boil. Take off the heat and stir in the cream, seeds, peel, sultanas, cherries, almonds and flour. Mix until evenly combined. Put heaped teaspoonfuls on to the prepared baking sheets, spaced well apart to allow for spreading.
3 Bake one sheet at a time, for 6–8 minutes, until the biscuits have spread considerably and the edges are golden brown. Using a large plain metal biscuit cutter, push the edges into the centre to create neat rounds. Bake for a further 2 minutes or until deep golden. Leave on the baking sheet for 2 minutes, then transfer to a wire rack and leave to cool completely.
4 Melt the chocolate in a heatproof bowl set over a pan of gently simmering water, making sure the base of the bowl doesn't touch the water, stirring occasionally. Spread on the underside of each Florentine and mark wavy lines with a fork. Put, chocolate-side up, on a sheet of baking parchment and leave to set.

TO STORE
Store in an airtight container. They will keep for up to two weeks.

ORANGE TUILE BISCUITS

MAKE 24

Preparation: 10 minutes, plus chilling
Cooking time: 12 minutes per batch, plus cooling

3 large egg whites
100g (3½oz) icing sugar, sifted
100g (3½oz) plain flour
finely grated zest of 1 orange
75g (3oz) unsalted butter, melted

PER BISCUIT

55 cals; 3g fat (of which 2g saturates); 8g carbohydrate; 0.1g salt

1 Put the egg whites into a clean, grease-free bowl, add the sugar and whisk lightly. Stir in the flour, orange zest and melted butter, then cover and chill for 30 minutes.
2 Preheat the oven to 200°C (180°C fan oven) mark 6. Line a baking sheet with baking parchment.
3 Put 3 teaspoonfuls of the mixture, spaced well apart, on the prepared baking sheet and spread out into 9cm (3½ inch) circles.
4 Bake for 12 minutes or until just brown around the edges. Remove from the oven and, while still warm, shape each biscuit over a rolling pin to curl. Repeat with the remaining mixture. Leave on a wire rack to cool completely.

TO STORE
Store in an airtight container. They will keep for up to one week.

AMARETTI BISCUITS

MAKES ABOUT 24

Preparation: 5 minutes
Cooking time: 20 minutes, plus cooling

125g (4oz) ground almonds
15g (½oz) ground rice
225g (8oz) caster sugar
2 medium egg whites
½ tsp almond flavouring
about 24 split almonds

PER BISCUIT

79 calories; 4g fat (of which 0.3g saturates); 11g carbohydrate; 0.1g salt

1 Preheat the oven to 180°C (160°C fan oven) mark 4. Line two
   baking sheets with rice paper.
2 Mix together the ground almonds, ground rice and sugar. Add
   the egg whites and almond flavouring and beat together until
   smooth.
3 Put the mixture into a piping bag fitted with a 1cm (½ inch)
   plain nozzle. Pipe small rounds about 2.5cm (1 inch) in
   diameter on to the paper, leaving plenty of room for spreading.
   Top each biscuit with a split almond.
4 Bake in the oven for about 20 minutes until pale golden brown.
   Transfer to a wire rack and leave to cool. Remove the rice
   paper from around each amaretti before serving.

TO STORE

Store in an airtight container. They will keep for up to two weeks.

HAZELNUT AND CHOCOLATE BISCOTTI

• •

MAKES ABOUT 28

Preparation: 10 minutes
Cooking time: 35–40 minutes, plus cooling

125g (4oz) plain flour, sifted, plus extra to dust
75g (3oz) golden caster sugar
¼ tsp baking powder
pinch of cinnamon
pinch of salt
1 large egg, beaten
1 tbsp milk
¼ tsp vanilla extract
25g (1oz) hazelnuts
25g (1oz) plain chocolate chips

PER BISCUIT

50 cals; 1g fat (of which trace saturates); 9g carbohydrate; 0g salt

1 Preheat the oven to 200°C (180°C fan oven) mark 6. Put the flour into a large bowl. Stir in the sugar, baking powder, cinnamon and salt. Make a well in the centre and, using a fork, stir in the beaten egg, milk, vanilla extract, hazelnuts and chocolate chips to form a sticky dough.

2 Turn out the dough on to a lightly floured surface and gently knead into a ball. Roll into a 28cm (11 inch) log shape. Put on a non-stick baking sheet and flatten slightly. Bake for 20–25 minutes until pale golden.

3 Lower the oven setting to 150°C (130°C fan oven) mark 2. Transfer the biscotti log on to a chopping board and slice diagonally with a bread knife at 1cm (½ inch) intervals. Arrange the slices on the baking sheet and put back into the oven for 15 minutes or until golden and dry. Transfer to a wire rack and leave to cool completely.

TO STORE

Store in an airtight container. They will keep for up to one month.

NOTES

• To enjoy Italian-style, dunk in coffee or dessert wine.
• To make as gifts, divide the biscuits among four large squares of cellophane, then draw up the edges and tie with ribbon. Label the packages with storage information and an eat-by date.

CHOCOLATE FUDGE SHORTBREAD

● ●

CUTS INTO 20 SQUARES

Preparation: 30 minutes
Cooking time: 20 minutes, plus cooling
and setting

175g (6oz) unsalted butter, at room temperature, diced, plus extra
   to grease
250g (9oz) plain flour, plus extra to dust
75g (3oz) golden caster sugar

TOPPING

2 x 397g cans sweetened condensed milk
100g (3½oz) light muscovado sugar
100g (3½oz) butter
250g (9oz) plain chocolate (at least 70% cocoa solids), broken
   into pieces

PER SQUARE

369 cals; 19g fat (of which 12g saturates); 48g carbohydrate; 0.4g salt

1　Preheat the oven to 180°C (160°C fan oven) mark 4. Grease
   a 33 x 23cm (13 x 9 inch) Swiss roll tin and line with baking
   parchment.
2　Put the flour, caster sugar and butter into a food processor
   and blend until the mixture forms crumbs, then pulse a little
   more until it forms a ball. Turn out on to a lightly floured
   surface and knead lightly to combine. Press the mixture into
   the prepared tin.
3　Bake for 20 minutes or until firm to the touch and a very pale
   brown.
4　To make the topping, put the condensed milk, muscovado
   sugar and butter into a non-stick pan and cook over a medium
   heat, stirring continuously until a fudge-like consistency.
   (Alternatively, melt in a heatproof bowl in a 900W microwave
   oven on full power for 12 minutes or until the mixture is thick
   and fudgy, beating with a whisk every 2–3 minutes.) Spoon the
   caramel on to the shortbread, smooth over and leave to cool.
5　To finish, melt the chocolate in a heatproof bowl set over a pan
   of gently simmering water, making sure the base of the bowl
   doesn't touch the water, then pour over the caramel layer.
   Leave to set at room temperature, then cut into 20 squares
   to serve.

TO STORE

Store in an airtight container. They will keep for up to one week.

SHORTBREAD

• •

MAKES 18–20

Preparation: 20 minutes, plus chilling
Cooking time: 15–20 minutes, plus cooling

225g (8oz) butter, at room temperature
125g (4oz) golden caster sugar
225g (8oz) plain flour
125g (4oz) rice flour
pinch of salt
golden or coloured granulated sugar to coat
caster sugar to sprinkle

PER PIECE

190–170 cals; 10–9g fat (of which 7–6g saturates);23–21g carbohydrate; 0.3–0.2g salt

1 Cream the butter and sugar together in a bowl until pale and fluffy. Sift the flours and salt together on to the creamed mixture and stir in, using a wooden spoon, until the mixture resembles breadcrumbs.

2 Gather the dough together with your hand and turn on to a clean surface. Knead very lightly until it forms a ball, then lightly roll into a sausage, about 5cm (2 inch) thick. Wrap in clingfilm and chill in the fridge until firm.

3 Preheat the oven to 190°C (170°C fan oven) mark 5. Line two baking sheets with greaseproof paper. Remove the clingfilm and slice the dough into discs, 7–10mm (⅓–½ inch) thick. Pour some granulated sugar on to a plate and roll the edge of each disc in the sugar. Put the shortbread, cut-side up, on the baking sheets.

4 Bake the shortbread for 15–20 minutes, depending on thickness, until very pale golden. On removing from the oven, sprinkle with caster sugar. Leave on the baking sheets for 10 minutes, then transfer to a wire rack and leave to cool.

TO STORE
Store in an airtight container. They will keep for up to two weeks.

CHEESECAKES, TORTES AND NO-BAKE CAKES

CLASSIC BAKED CHEESECAKE

LONG CHILLING REQUIRED

CUTS INTO 12 SLICES

Preparation: 30 minutes, plus chilling
Cooking time: 55 minutes, plus cooling and chilling

BASE
125g (4oz) unsalted butter, melted, plus extra to grease
250g pack digestive biscuits, finely crushed (see page 307)

FILLING
2 large lemons
2 x 250g cartons curd cheese
142ml carton soured cream
2 medium eggs
175g (6oz) golden caster sugar
1 ½ tsp vanilla extract
1 tbsp cornflour
50g (2oz) sultanas

PER SLICE
340 cals; 19g fat (of which 11g saturates); 36g carbohydrate; 1g salt

1 Grease a 20.5cm (8 inch) springform cake tin. Put the biscuits into a bowl, add the melted butter and mix until well combined. Tip the crumb mixture into the prepared tin and press evenly on to the bottom, using the back of a metal spoon to level the surface. Chill for 1 hour or until firm.

2 Preheat the oven to 180°C (160°C fan oven) mark 4. To make the filling, grate the zest from 1 of the lemons and set aside. Halve the same lemon and squeeze out the juice. Halve the other lemon and cut into very thin slices.

3 Put the lemon zest, lemon juice, curd cheese, soured cream, eggs, sugar, vanilla extract and cornflour into a large bowl. Using a hand-held electric whisk, beat together until thick and smooth, then fold in the sultanas. Pour the mixture into the tin and shake gently to level the surface.

4 Bake for 30 minutes. Put the lemon slices, overlapping, on top. Bake for a further 20–25 minutes until the cheesecake is just set and golden brown. Turn off the oven and leave the cheesecake inside, with the door ajar, until it is cool, then chill for at least 2 hours or overnight.

5 Remove the cheesecake from the fridge about 30 minutes before serving. Run a knife around the edge, release the clasp on the tin and remove the cake. Cut the cheesecake into slices to serve.

ORANGE AND CHOCOLATE CHEESECAKE

LONG CHILLING REQUIRED

CUTS INTO 12 SLICES

Preparation: 45 minutes

Cooking time: 2–2¼ hours, plus cooling and chilling

225g (8oz) chilled unsalted butter, plus
   extra to grease
250g (9oz) plain flour, sifted
150g (5oz) light muscovado sugar
3 tbsp cocoa powder
chocolate curls to decorate (see page 40,
   optional)

TOPPING
2 oranges
800g (1lb 12oz) cream cheese
250g (9oz) mascarpone cheese
4 large eggs
225g (8oz) golden caster sugar
2 tbsp cornflour
½ tsp vanilla extract
1 vanilla pod

PER SLICE
767 cals; 60g fat (of which 37g saturates);
53g carbohydrate; 1.2g salt

1 Preheat the oven to 180°C (160°C fan oven) mark 4. Grease a 23cm (9 inch) springform cake tin and base-line with baking parchment.
2 Cut 175g (6oz) butter into cubes. Melt the remaining butter and set aside. Put the flour and cubed butter into a food processor with the sugar and cocoa powder. Whiz until the texture of fine breadcrumbs. (Alternatively, rub the butter into the flour in a large bowl by hand or using a pastry cutter. Stir in the sugar and cocoa powder.) Pour in the melted butter and pulse, or stir with a fork, until the mixture comes together.
3 Tip the crumb mixture into the prepared tin and press evenly on to the bottom, using the back of a metal spoon to level the surface. Bake for 35–40 minutes until lightly puffed; avoid over-browning or the biscuit base will have a bitter flavour. Remove from the oven and leave to cool. Lower the oven setting to 150°C (130°C fan oven) mark 2.
4 Meanwhile, make the topping. Grate the zest from the oranges, then squeeze the juice – you will need 150ml (¼ pint). Put the cream cheese, mascarpone, eggs, sugar, cornflour, grated orange zest and vanilla extract into a large bowl. Using a hand-held electric whisk, beat the ingredients together thoroughly until well combined.
5 Split the vanilla pod in half lengthways and, using the tip of a sharp knife, scrape out the seeds and add them to the cheese mixture. Beat in the orange juice and continue whisking until the mixture is smooth.
6 Pour the cheese mixture over the cooled biscuit base. Bake for about 1½ hours until pale golden on top, slightly risen and just set around the edge. The cheesecake should still be slightly wobbly in the middle; it will set as it cools. Turn off the oven and leave the cheesecake inside, with the door ajar, to cool for 1 hour. Remove and allow to cool completely (about 3 hours), then chill.
7 Just before serving, unclip the tin and transfer the cheesecake to a plate. Scatter chocolate curls on top to decorate, if you like.

CHOCOLATE TORTE

CUTS INTO 10 SLICES

Preparation: 15 minutes, plus chilling
Cooking time: 5 minutes, plus cooling

200g (7oz) plain chocolate, broken into pieces
25g (1oz) butter, melted, plus extra to grease
1½ tbsp golden syrup
125g (4oz) butter biscuits, finely crushed (see page 307)
40g (1½oz) icing sugar
300ml (½ pint) double cream, at room temperature
2–3 tbsp Amaretto liqueur (optional)
crème fraîche to serve

DECORATION
plain chocolate, grated
raspberries
icing sugar to dust

PER SERVING
383 cals; 27g fat (of which 16g saturates); 31g carbohydrate; 0.2g salt

1 Melt the chocolate pieces in a heatproof bowl set over a pan
   of barely simmering water, making sure the base of the bowl
   doesn't touch the water. Put to one side to cool for 10 minutes.
   Grease a 20.5cm (8 inch) loose-bottomed cake tin and line the
   sides with greaseproof paper.
2 In a medium bowl, mix together the butter, golden syrup and
   crushed biscuits. Press the mixture into the bottom of the
   prepared tin.
3 Sift the icing sugar into a separate bowl. Pour in the cream and
   Amaretto, if you like, and whip until the cream just holds its
   shape. Using a metal spoon, fold the cooled chocolate into the
   cream mixture. Spoon the chocolate mixture into the cake tin,
   level the surface, cover and chill until ready to serve.
4 Transfer the torte to a serving plate and peel off the paper.
   Scatter grated chocolate over the top, dot a few raspberries
   over and lightly dust with icing sugar. Serve in slices with
   crème fraîche.

NOTE
For convenience, prepare ahead. Complete the recipe to the end
of step 3 up to one day ahead. Complete the recipe to serve.

LUXURY CHOCOLATE ORANGE TORTE

CUTS INTO 12 SLICES

Preparation: 30 minutes

Cooking time: 55 minutes–1 hour 5 minutes, plus cooling

75g (3oz) unsalted butter, diced, plus extra to grease
100g (3½oz) plain chocolate (at least 70% cocoa solids), broken
   into pieces
6 medium eggs
225g (8oz) golden caster sugar
150g (5oz) ground almonds, sifted
grated zest and juice of 1 orange
strawberries and raspberries to serve

PER SLICE

231 cals; 12g fat (of which 3g saturates); 25g carbohydrate; 0.1g salt

1 Preheat the oven to 190°C (170°C fan oven) mark 5. Grease
   a 20.5cm (8 inch) springform cake tin and line with
   greaseproof paper.
2 Melt the butter and chocolate in a heatproof bowl set over a
   pan of gently simmering water, making sure the base of the
   bowl doesn't touch the water. Remove the bowl from the pan
   and set aside to cool a little.
3 Put the eggs and sugar into a large bowl and mix with a
   hand-held electric whisk until the volume has tripled and the
   mixture is thick and foamy – it will take 5–10 minutes. Add the
   ground almonds, orange zest and juice to the egg mixture, then
   gently fold together with a metal spoon.
4 Pour about two-thirds of the mixture into the prepared tin.
   Add the melted chocolate and butter to the remaining
   mixture and fold together. Add to the tin and swirl around just
   once or twice to create a marbled effect. Bake for 50 minutes–
   1 hour. Leave to cool in the tin.
5 Carefully remove the cake from the tin and slice. Serve with
   strawberries and raspberries.

TO STORE
Store in an airtight container. It will keep for up to three days.

PASTRY

BASIC PASTRY RECIPES

· ·

SHORTCRUST PASTRY

MAKES 225G (8OZ)
Preparation: 10 minutes, plus chilling

225g (8oz) plain flour, plus extra to dust
pinch of salt
125g (4oz) unsalted butter, or half white vegetable fat and half butter, cut into pieces

PER 25G (1OZ)
110 cals; 6g fat (of which 3g saturates); 12g carbohydrate; 0.6g salt

1   Sift the flour and salt into a bowl, add the fat and mix lightly. Using your fingertips, rub the fat into the flour until the mixture resembles fine breadcrumbs.
2   Sprinkle 3–4 tbsp cold water evenly over the surface and stir with a round-bladed knife until the mixture begins to stick together in large lumps. If the dough seems dry, add a little extra water. With one hand, collect the dough together to form a ball.
3   Knead lightly on a lightly floured surface for a few seconds to form a smooth, firm dough; do not over-work. Form the pastry into a ball, wrap tightly in clingfilm and leave to rest in the fridge for at least 30 minutes before rolling out. (This allows the pastry to 'relax' and prevents shrinkage when it is baked.)

NOTES
- To make the pastry in a food processor, put the flour and salt in the processor bowl with the butter. Whiz until the mixture resembles fine crumbs, then add the water. Process briefly, using the pulse button, until the mixture just comes together in a ball. Continue from step 3.
- Shortcrust pastry can be stored in the fridge for up to three days, or frozen.

VARIATIONS
Wholemeal pastry:
Replace half the white flour with wholemeal flour. A little extra water may be needed to mix the dough.

Nut pastry:
Replace 50g (2oz) flour with finely chopped or ground walnuts, hazelnuts or almonds, adding them to the rubbed-in mixture just before the cold water.

Cheese pastry:
Stir in 3–4 tbsp freshly grated Parmesan or 75g (3oz) finely grated Cheddar cheese and a small pinch of mustard powder before adding the water.

Herb pastry:
Stir in 3 tbsp finely chopped fresh herbs, such as parsley, sage, thyme or rosemary, before adding the water.

· ·

SWEET SHORTCRUST PASTRY

MAKES 125G (4OZ)
Preparation: 10 minutes, plus chilling

125g (4oz) plain flour, plus extra to dust
pinch of salt
50g (2oz) unsalted butter, at room temperature, cut into pieces
2 medium egg yolks
50g (2oz) caster sugar

PER 25G (1OZ)
110 cals; 6g fat (of which 4g saturates); 14g carbohydrate; 0.5g salt

1   Sift the flour and salt into a mound on a clean surface. Make a large well in the centre and add the butter, egg yolks and sugar.
2   Using the fingertips of one hand, work the sugar, butter and egg yolks together until well blended.
3   Gradually work in all the flour to bind the mixture together.
4   Knead the dough gently on a lightly floured surface until smooth, then wrap in clingfilm and leave to rest in the fridge for at least 30 minutes before rolling out.

NOTE
This pastry can be stored in the fridge for up to three days, or frozen.

RICH SHORTCRUST PASTRY

MAKES 225G (8OZ)

Preparation: 10 minutes, plus chilling

125g (4oz) plain flour, plus extra to dust
pinch of salt
75g (3oz) unsalted butter or block margarine and lard, diced
1 tsp caster sugar
1 medium egg, beaten

PER 25G (1OZ)

120 cals; 5g fat (of which 2g saturates); 13g carbohydrate; 0.5g salt

1 Put the flour and salt into a bowl. Rub the fat into the flour until the mixture resembles fine breadcrumbs. Stir in the sugar.
2 Add the egg, stirring with a round-bladed knife until the ingredients begin to stick together in large lumps.
3 With one hand, collect the mixture together and knead lightly for a few seconds to give a firm, smooth dough. Form into a ball, wrap tightly in clingfilm and chill for 1 hour before using. Roll out the pastry on a lightly floured surface to make a sheet at least 5cm (2inch) larger than the tart tin or pie dish.

FLAKY (ROUGH PUFF) PASTRY

MAKES 225G (8OZ)

Preparation: 25 minutes, plus chilling

225g (8oz) plain flour, plus extra to dust
pinch of salt
175g (6oz) unsalted butter, chilled
1 tsp lemon juice

PER 25G (1OZ)

100 cals; 7g fat (of which 4g saturates); 9g carbohydrate; 0.6g salt

1 Sift the flour and salt together into a bowl. Cut the butter into 2cm (¾ inch) cubes and add to the flour. Mix lightly to coat the pieces of butter with flour.
2 Using a round-bladed knife, stir in 100ml (3½fl oz) chilled water together with the lemon juice to make a soft elastic dough. If the pastry is too dry, add a little extra water.
3 Turn out on to a lightly floured surface and lightly knead the dough until smooth.

4 Roll the pastry out to a neat rectangle, measuring 30.5 × 10cm (12 × 4 inch). Mark off three equal sections from top to bottom.
5 Fold the bottom third up and the top third down, then give the pastry a quarter turn, so that the folded edges are at the sides. Press the edges with a rolling pin to seal. Wrap in clingfilm and leave to rest in the fridge for 15 minutes.
6 Put the pastry on a lightly floured surface with the folded edges to the sides. Repeat the rolling, folding and turning sequence four more times. Wrap in clingfilm and leave to rest in the fridge for 30 minutes before rolling out.
7 Shape the rough puff pastry as required, then rest in the fridge for 30 minutes before baking.

NOTE
Rough puff pastry has the buttery flakiness of puff pastry, although it won't rise as much.

BASIC PASTRY RECIPES

PUFF PASTRY

MAKES 450G (1LB)

Preparation: 40 minutes, plus chilling

450g (1lb) strong plain (bread) flour, plus extra to dust
pinch of salt
450g (1lb) unsalted butter, chilled
1 tbsp lemon juice

PER 25G (1OZ)

100 cals; 8g fat (of which 4g saturates); 7g carbohydrate; 0.6g salt

1 Sift the flour and salt together into a bowl. Cut off 50g (2oz) butter and flatten the remaining large block with a rolling pin to a slab, about 2cm (¾ inch) thick; put to one side.
2 Cut the 50g (2oz) butter into small pieces and rub into the flour, using your fingertips.
3 Using a round-bladed knife, stir in the lemon juice and enough chilled water – you will need about 300ml (½ pint) – to make a soft elastic dough.
4 Turn out on to a lightly floured surface and quickly knead the dough until smooth. Cut a cross through half the depth, then open out to form a star.

5 Roll out, keeping the centre four times as thick as the flaps. Put the slab of butter in the centre of the dough. Fold the flaps over the dough, envelope-style.
6 Press gently with a rolling pin and roll out to a rectangle, measuring 40.5 x 20.5cm (16 x 8 inch).
7 Fold the bottom third up and the top third down, keeping the edges straight. Wrap in clingfilm and leave to rest in the fridge for 30 minutes.
8 Put the pastry on a lightly floured surface with the folded edges to the sides. Repeat the rolling, folding, resting and turning sequence five times.
9 Shape the puff pastry as required, then rest in the fridge for about 30 minutes before baking.

NOTES

- If possible, the pastry should be made the day before it is to be used. It is not practical to make less than a 450g (1lb) flour weight quantity.
- Ready-made puff pastry is available fresh and frozen, so use this for convenience, if you prefer. Two 375g (13oz) packs would be roughly equivalent to this home-made quantity.

HOT WATER CRUST PASTRY

MAKES 300G (11OZ)

Preparation: 10 minutes, plus resting

300g (11oz) plain flour
¼ tsp salt
65g (2½oz) white vegetable fat

PER 25G (1OZ)

80 cals; 3g fat (of which 1g saturates); 10g carbohydrate; 0.5g salt

1 Sift the flour and salt into a bowl and make a well in the middle.
2 Put the fat and 150ml (¼ pint) water in a small pan and heat slowly until the fat melts, then increase the heat and bring to the boil.

3 Pour the hot liquid into the flour well. Gradually lap the flour into the liquid, then beat together.
4 Lightly knead against the side of the bowl until smooth. Wrap the dough in a teatowel and leave to rest in a warm place for 20 minutes. Use the pastry while it is still warm and pliable.

NOTE

Any pastry not in use must be kept covered with a damp teatowel in a warm place (if exposed to air it will become dry and impossible to use).

CHOUX PASTRY

MAKES A 2-EGG QUANTITY
Preparation: 10 minutes

65g (2½oz) plain flour
pinch of salt
50g (2oz) unsalted butter
2 medium eggs, lightly beaten

PER 25G (1OZ)
50 cals; 4g fat (of which 2g saturates); 3g carbohydrate; 0.4g salt

1 Sift the flour and salt on to a large sheet of greaseproof paper.
2 Pour 150ml (¼ pint) cold water into a medium pan, add the butter and melt over a low heat. Increase the heat and bring to a rolling boil.
3 Take off the heat, immediately tip in all the flour and beat vigorously, using a wooden spoon. Continue beating until the mixture is smooth and leaves the sides of the pan to form a ball; do not over-beat. Leave to cool slightly, for 1–2 minutes.
4 Gradually add the eggs, beating well between each addition, adding just enough to give a smooth dropping consistency. The choux pastry should be smooth and shiny. Use as required.

NOTE
For a sweeter pastry, add 1 tsp caster sugar with the flour and salt.

PIZZA BASE DOUGH

MAKES 1 LARGE OR 2 SMALL PIZZA BASES
Preparation: 5 minutes, plus rising

225g (8oz) strong plain (bread) flour, plus extra to dust
½ tsp sea salt
1 tsp fast-action dried yeast
1 tbsp extra virgin olive oil, plus extra to grease

PER 25G (1OZ)
60 cals; 1g fat (of which 0.3g saturates); 11g carbohydrate; 0.8g salt

1 Sift the flour and salt into a bowl and stir in the dried yeast. Make a well in the centre and gradually work in 150ml (¼ pint) warm water and the olive oil to form a soft dough.
2 Turn the pizza dough out on to a lightly floured surface and knead well for 8–10 minutes until smooth and elastic. (Alternatively, use a large food mixer fitted with a dough hook.)
3 Put into an oiled bowl, turn the dough once to coat the surface with oil and cover the bowl with clingfilm. Leave to rise in a warm place for about 1 hour until doubled in size.
4 Knock back the dough and shape as required.

NOTE
If preferred, use 15g (½oz) fresh yeast instead of fast-action dried yeast. Mix with 2 tbsp of the flour, a pinch of sugar and the warm water. Leave in a warm place for 10 minutes until frothy, then add to the rest of the flour and salt. Mix to a dough and continue as above.

TOPPINGS
Scatter one or two of the following on top of a basic cheese and tomato pizza:
- Bacon or pancetta bits, or slices of prosciutto
- Rocket leaves
- Dried chilli flakes
- Capers
- Sliced sun-dried tomatoes
- Pepperoni slices
- Roasted peppers
- Artichoke hearts, drained and quartered
- Sliced mushrooms

SPINACH AND FETA PIE

● ●

SERVES 10

Preparation: 40 minutes
Cooking time: 45 minutes, plus cooling

1 tbsp vegetable oil
1 onion, peeled and finely chopped
1 garlic clove, peeled and crushed
1 tbsp cumin seeds
400g (14oz) baby leaf spinach
1.1kg (2½lb) waxy potatoes, such as Desirée, boiled in their skins until
    tender, cooled, peeled and sliced
2 x 200g packs vegetarian feta cheese, crumbled
2 medium eggs, beaten
50g (2oz) butter, melted, plus extra for greasing
200g pack filo pastry, thawed if frozen
salt and ground black pepper

PER SERVING

311 cals; 15g fat (of which 9g saturates); 33g carbohydrate; 1.7g salt

1 Heat the oil in a large pan and cook the onion for 10 minutes or until soft. Add the
   garlic and cumin and cook for 1–2 minutes. Add the spinach, cover and cook until the
   spinach has just wilted – 1–2 minutes. Tip into a bowl and leave to cool. Add the
   potatoes, cheese and eggs. Season and mix.
2 Preheat the oven to 200°C (180°C fan oven) mark 6. Lightly grease a 28cm (11 inch)
   tart tin with butter. Unroll the pastry and cut the sheets lengthways into three. Work
   with one-third of the strips at a time and cover the remainder with clingfilm. Lay a
   strip on the tin, starting from the middle so that half covers the tin and half hangs
   over the edge. Brush with melted butter, then lay another strip next to it, slightly
   overlapping, and brush again. Repeat, working quickly around the tin in a cartwheel
   shape.
3 Add the filling and level the surface. Fold in the overhanging pastry to cover the
   mixture, filling any gaps with leftover pastry. Drizzle with the remaining melted butter,
   then cook for 45 minutes or until golden.

NOTE
If you don't eat all the pie, it's just
as delicious cold the next day or, if
you prefer, warm it in the oven at
200°C (180°C fan oven) mark 6 for
15–20 minutes. Cover with foil if it
starts to over-brown.

CHICKEN AND MUSHROOM PIES

SERVES 4

Preparation: 20 minutes, plus chilling

Cooking time: 55 minutes–1 hour 5 minutes, plus cooling

2 tbsp olive oil

1 leek, about 200g (7oz), finely sliced

2–3 garlic cloves, peeled and crushed

350g (12oz) boneless, skinless chicken thighs, cut into
   2.5cm (1 inch) cubes

200g (7oz) chestnut mushrooms, sliced

150ml (¼ pint) double cream

2 tbsp freshly chopped thyme

500g pack puff pastry, thawed if frozen

plain flour to dust

1 medium egg, beaten

salt and ground black pepper

PER SERVING

805 cals; 58g fat (of which 14g saturates); 49g carbohydrate; 1.2g salt

1 Heat the oil in a pan and fry the leek over a medium heat for
   5 minutes to soften. Add the garlic and cook for 1 minute.
   Add the chicken pieces and continue to cook for 8–10
   minutes. Add the mushrooms and cook for 5 minutes or until
   all the juices have disappeared.

2 Pour the cream into the pan and bring to the boil. Cook for
   5 minutes to make a thick sauce. Add the thyme, then season
   well with salt and pepper. Tip into a bowl and leave to cool.

3 Roll out the pastry on a lightly floured surface until it measures
   33 x 33cm (13 x 13 inch). Cut into four squares. Brush the
   edges with water and spoon the chicken mixture into the
   middle of each square. Bring each corner of the square up to
   the middle to make a parcel. Crimp the edges to seal, leaving a
   small hole in the middle. Brush the pies with beaten egg, put
   on a baking sheet and chill for 20 minutes.

4 Preheat the oven to 200°C (180°C fan oven) mark 6. Cook
   the pies for 30–40 minutes until golden.

VARIATION

For a vegetarian alternative, replace the chicken with 200g (7oz)
cooked, peeled (or vacuum-packed) chestnuts, roughly chopped.
Add another leek and increase the quantity of mushrooms to
300g (11oz).

LEEK AND HAM GALETTE

• • • • • • • • • • • • • • • • • • •

SERVES 4

Preparation: 30 minutes, plus chilling

Cooking time: 40 minutes, plus cooling

25g (1oz) butter, plus extra to grease
350g (12oz) medium leeks, trimmed and cut into
  2cm (¾ inch) thick slices
25g (1oz) plain flour, plus extra to dust
50ml (2fl oz) milk
1 tbsp freshly chopped marjoram
50g (2oz) Gruyère cheese, cubed, plus 2 tbsp, grated
150g (5oz) cooked sliced ham, thickly shredded
225g (8oz) puff pastry, thawed if frozen
½ medium egg, beaten with a pinch of salt
salt and freshly ground black pepper

PER SERVING

395 cals; 25g fat (of which 6g saturates); 29g carbohydrate; 2g salt

1 Grease a baking sheet. Cook the leeks in lightly salted boiling water for 2–3 minutes until just beginning to soften. Drain, keeping the cooking liquid to one side. Plunge the leeks into cold water, drain and dry well on kitchen paper.

2 Melt the butter in a pan, remove from the heat and mix in the flour to form a smooth paste. Add 225ml (8fl oz) leek water and the milk and stir until smooth. Bring to the boil, then reduce the heat and simmer for 1–2 minutes. Remove from the heat, cover and leave to cool for 20 minutes or until cold. Add the marjoram, leeks, cubed cheese and ham and season.

3 Roll out the pastry on a lightly floured surface to a 30.5 × 33cm (12 × 13 inch) rectangle. Cut into two rectangles, one 15 × 30.5cm (6 × 12 inch) and the other 18 × 30.5cm (7 × 12 inch). Put the smaller piece on to the baking sheet. Spoon on the ham mixture, leaving a 2cm (¾ inch) border all the way around. Brush the border with beaten egg. Cover the filling with the larger pastry rectangle and press the edges together. Cut slashes in the top of the pastry to prevent the filling seeping out. Crimp the edges to seal, then cover and freeze for 20 minutes or until firm.

4 Preheat the oven to 220°C (200°C fan oven) mark 7. Remove the galettes from the freezer, brush again with the beaten egg and sprinkle with the grated cheese. Bake for 20–30 minutes until brown and crisp. Serve hot.

FREEZING TIP

To freeze, cover the uncooked galette in clingfilm and freeze on the baking sheet. When firm, remove from the baking tray. Wrap in baking parchment, and then in clingfilm. To use, thaw for 3 hours at cool room temperature on baking parchment. Preheat the oven to 220°C (200°C fan oven) mark 7 and put a baking tray in the oven to heat. Brush the galette with beaten egg and sprinkle with cheese. Put the galette on the hot tray (this will keep the pastry base crisp) and bake for 40 minutes.

QUICHE LORRAINE

SERVES 8

Preparation: 35 minutes, plus chilling

Cooking time: 1 hour

Shortcrust Pastry (see page 138), made with 200g (7oz) plain flour,
    pinch of salt, 100g (3½oz) chilled butter and 1 large egg
plain flour to dust

FILLING

5 large eggs
225g (8oz) unsmoked streaky bacon, rind removed
40g (1½oz) butter
125g (4oz) shallots, onions or spring onions, peeled and finely chopped
400g (14oz) crème fraîche
100g (3½oz) Gruyère cheese, grated
salt and ground black pepper
crispy bacon and fried spring onions to garnish

PER SERVING

595 cals; 50g fat (of which 29g saturates); 22g carbohydrate; 1.5g salt

1 Preheat the oven to 200°C (180°C fan oven) mark 6. Roll out the pastry thinly on a lightly floured surface and use to line a 23cm (9 inch), 3cm (1¼ inch) deep, loose-based tart tin. Bake the pastry case blind (see page 323). Meanwhile, lightly whisk the eggs for the filling. Use a little to brush the inside of the pastry case and return it to the oven for 5 minutes to seal any cracks. Lower the oven setting to 190°C (170°C fan oven) mark 5.

2 Cut the bacon into 5mm (¼ inch) strips. Put the bacon in a pan of cold water and bring to the boil. Drain, then refresh under cold water and dry on kitchen paper.

3 Melt the butter in a frying pan, add the shallots or onions and cook for 1 minute. Add the bacon and cook, stirring, until brown.

4 Mix the eggs with the crème fraîche and cheese and season. Put the bacon mixture in the pastry case and spoon the crème fraîche mixture on top (see note). Cook for 30–35 minutes until golden and just set. Cool for 10 minutes before serving. Garnish with bacon and fried spring onions.

NOTE
Fill the pastry case as full as possible. You may find you have a little mixture left, as flan tins vary in size.

PLUM AND ALMOND TART

● ●

CUTS INTO 8 SLICES

Preparation: 30 minutes, plus chilling

Cooking time: 40 minutes, plus cooling and setting

150g (5oz) unsalted butter, chilled and diced

175g (6oz) plain flour, plus extra to dust

7 tbsp soured cream

FILLING

50g (2oz) unsalted butter

50g (2oz) caster sugar, plus extra to dust

2 medium eggs, lightly beaten

100g (3½oz) ground almonds

1 tbsp Kirsch or 3–4 drops almond essence

900g (2lb) plums, stoned and quartered

50g (2oz) blanched almonds to decorate

175g (6oz) redcurrant jelly

PER SLICE

535 cals; 35g fat (of which 16g saturates); 50g carbohydrate; 0.5g salt

1 To make the pastry, put the butter and flour into a food processor and whiz for
   1–2 seconds. Add the soured cream and process for a further 1–2 seconds until the
   dough just begins to come together. (Alternatively, rub the butter into the flour in a
   large bowl by hand or using a pastry cutter, then mix in the soured cream.) Turn out
   on to a lightly floured surface and knead lightly for about 30 seconds until the pastry
   just comes together. Wrap in clingfilm and chill for 30 minutes.

2 To make the filling, put the butter into a bowl and beat until soft, then add the sugar
   and beat until light and fluffy. Beat in the eggs, alternating with the ground almonds.
   Add the Kirsch or almond essence, cover and set aside.

3 Roll out the pastry on a lightly floured surface to a 30.5cm (12 inch) circle, then
   transfer to a baking sheet and prick all over with a fork. Spread the almond mixture
   over the pastry, leaving a 3cm (1¼ inch) border all round. Scatter the plums over the
   filling and fold the edges of the pastry up over the fruit. Dust with caster sugar, then
   chill for 20 minutes.

4 Preheat the oven to 220°C (200°C fan oven) mark 7 and put a baking tray in the
   oven to heat for 10 minutes. Put the tart, on its baking sheet, on top of the hot baking
   tray. Cook for 35–40 minutes until deep golden brown.

5 Leave the tart to cool for 10 minutes, then slide it on to a wire rack. Arrange the
   almonds among the fruit. Heat the redcurrant jelly gently in a pan, stirring until smooth,
   then brush generously over the tart. Leave to set.

PINENUT AND HONEY TART

●●●●●●●●●●●●●●●●●●●●●

CUTS INTO 6 SLICES

Preparation: 50 minutes, plus chilling

Cooking time: 1 hour, plus cooling

250g (9oz) plain flour, plus extra to dust
200g (7oz) unsalted butter, softened
40g (1½oz) icing sugar
4 large eggs
100g (3½oz) pinenuts
200g (7oz) muscovado sugar
100ml (3½fl oz) clear honey
150ml (¼ pint) double cream
ice cream to serve

PER SLICE

863 cals; 54g fat (of which 26g saturates); 88g carbohydrate; 0.6g salt

1 Put 225g (8oz) flour, 150g (5oz) butter and the icing sugar into a food processor and pulse until the mixture resembles fine crumbs. (Alternatively, rub the butter into the flour in a large bowl, by hand or using a pastry cutter, until it resembles fine crumbs. Stir in the icing sugar.) Add 1 egg. Pulse, or stir with a fork, until the mixture forms a ball. Wrap in clingfilm and chill for 30 minutes.

2 Preheat the oven to 200°C (180°C fan oven) mark 6. Roll out the pastry on a lightly floured surface and use to line a 23cm (9 inch) loose-based tart tin. Prick the base all over with a fork and bake blind (see page 323), using a little of the remaining eggs to seal the pastry case. Remove from the oven. Increase the oven setting to 190°C (170°C fan oven) mark 5.

3 Sprinkle 75g (3oz) pinenuts over the pastry base. Melt 25g (1oz) butter and whisk with 175g (6oz) muscovado sugar, the honey, remaining eggs and the cream. Pour into the pastry case and bake for 25–30 minutes.

4 Pulse the remaining pinenuts, flour, butter and sugar until the mixture forms a crumbly texture. (Alternatively, rub the butter into the flour in a large bowl and stir in the pinenuts and sugar.) When the tart is cooked, remove it from the oven, sprinkle with the crumble mixture and return to the oven for 8–10 minutes.

5 Remove from the oven and leave to cool slightly. Serve warm, with ice cream.

BRAMLEY APPLE AND CUSTARD TART

• •

CUTS INTO 12 SLICES

Preparation: 30 minutes, plus chilling
Cooking time: about 2 hours, plus cooling and chilling

750g (1lb 11oz) Bramley apples, peeled, cored and roughly chopped
200g (7oz) golden caster sugar
500g shortcrust pastry, chilled
plain flour to dust
a little beaten egg to seal the pastry case
400ml (14fl oz) double cream
1 cinnamon stick
3 large egg yolks, plus 1 large egg, beaten together
2 dessert apples to decorate
Apple Sauce (see below) to serve

PER SLICE

472 cals; 32g fat (of which 15g saturates); 46g carbohydrate; 0.5g salt

1 Cook the Bramley apples with 2 tbsp water over a low heat until soft. Add 50g (2oz) sugar and beat to make a purée. Leave to cool.

2 Roll out the pastry on a lightly floured surface and use to line a 20.5cm (8 inch), 4cm (1½ inch) deep, loose-based fluted flan tin. Cover and chill for 1 hour. Preheat the oven to 180°C (160°C fan oven) mark 4. Bake the pastry case blind (see page 323). Brush the inside with beaten egg and put back in the oven for 1 minute to seal. Remove from the oven.

3 Put the cream into a pan with 50g (2oz) sugar and the cinnamon stick. Bring slowly to the boil, then take off the heat and remove the cinnamon. Cool for 2–3 minutes, then beat in the egg yolks and egg.

4 Lower the oven setting to 170°C (150°C fan oven) mark 3. Put the tart on a baking sheet, then spoon the apple purée over the pastry. Pour the cream mixture on top and bake for 1–1½ hours until the custard is set. Remove from the oven, cool in the tin, then chill.

5 To decorate, preheat the grill. Cut the dessert apples into 5mm (¼ inch) thick slices and lay them on a lipped baking sheet. Sprinkle with 50g (2oz) sugar and grill for 4–5 minutes until caramelised. Turn them over and repeat on the other side, then cool. Remove the tart from the tin and decorate with the apple slices. Serve with Apple Sauce.

APPLE SAUCE

Pour 300ml (½ pint) apple juice into a measuring jug. Mix 2 tbsp of the apple juice with 1 tbsp arrowroot to make a smooth paste. Pour the remaining apple juice into a small pan and bring to a gentle simmer. Add the arrowroot paste and continue to heat, stirring constantly, for 2–3 minutes until the sauce has thickened slightly.

SWEET RICOTTA TART

CUTS INTO 8 SLICES

Preparation: 25 minutes, plus chilling
Cooking time: 1 hour, plus cooling

Sweet Shortcrust Pastry (see page 138), made with 200g (7oz) plain
   flour, 75g (3oz) unsalted butter, 50g (2oz) golden caster sugar and
   1 medium egg in place of the egg yolks
plain flour to dust
a little beaten egg to seal the pastry case
icing sugar to dust

FILLING
100g (3½oz) cracked wheat or bulgur wheat
200ml (7fl oz) milk
250g (9oz) ricotta cheese
150g (5oz) golden caster sugar
2 medium eggs
1 tbsp orange flower water
1 tsp vanilla extract
½ tsp ground cinnamon
1 piece – about 40g (1½oz) – candied peel, finely chopped

PER SLICE
404 cals; 15g fat (of which 9g saturates); 60g carbohydrate; 0.3g salt

1 To make the filling, put the wheat into a pan and add the milk, then cover and bring to
the boil. Reduce the heat and simmer for 5–8 minutes until all the liquid has been
absorbed and the wheat still has a slight bite. Leave to cool.

2 Preheat the oven to 190°C (170°C fan oven) mark 5. Roll out the pastry on a lightly
floured surface and use to line a 20.5cm (8 inch) loose-based sandwich tin. Prick the base
all over with a fork. Cover and chill for 10 minutes. Knead together the trimmings, then
wrap and chill. Bake the pastry case blind (see page 323). Brush with beaten egg and put
back in the oven for 1 minute to seal. Remove from the oven.

3 Put the ricotta into a bowl and add the sugar, eggs, orange flower water, vanilla extract
and cinnamon. Beat well. Add the peel and wheat and mix.

4 Roll out the pastry trimmings. Cut out six strips, each measuring 1 × 20.5cm (½ × 8 inch).
Pour the filling into the pastry case, then lay the strips on top. Bake for 45 minutes. Leave
in the tin for 10 minutes, then turn out on to a wire rack and leave to cool completely.
Dust with icing sugar to serve.

CARAMELISED ORANGE TART

CUTS INTO 8 SLICES

Preparation: 15 minutes, plus chilling
Cooking time: 45 minutes, plus cooling

PASTRY
225g (8oz) plain flour, plus extra to dust
pinch of salt
125g (4oz) unsalted butter, diced
2 tbsp golden icing sugar
1 medium egg yolk, beaten

FILLING
juice of 1 lemon
juice of 1 orange
zest of 2 oranges
75g (3oz) unsalted butter
225g (8oz) golden granulated sugar
3 medium eggs, beaten
75g (3oz) ground almonds
2 tbsp orange liqueur
a few drops of orange food colouring
    (optional)

DECORATION
100g (3½oz) golden caster sugar
pared zest of 1 orange, cut into slivers

PER SLICE
556 cals; 29g fat (of which 14g saturates);
70g carbohydrate; 0.5g salt

1   To make the pastry, put the flour, salt, butter and icing sugar into a food processor and pulse until the mixture forms fine crumbs. (Alternatively, rub the fat into the flour, by hand or using a pastry cutter, then stir in the icing sugar.) Beat the egg yolk with 2 tbsp cold water and add to the flour mixture. Process (or stir) until the crumbs make a dough. Knead lightly, wrap and chill for 30 minutes.

2   To make the filling, put the juices, orange zest, butter, sugar and eggs into a heavy-based pan and heat gently, stirring until thickened. Stir in the almonds, liqueur and food colouring, if you like, then set aside.

3   Preheat the oven to 200°C (180°C fan oven) mark 6. Roll out the dough on a lightly floured surface and use to line a 23cm (9 inch) tin. Prick the base all over with a fork. Cover and chill for 10 minutes. Bake the pastry case blind (see page 323). Remove from the oven. Lower the oven setting to 180°C (160°C fan oven) mark 4. Pour the filling into the pastry case and bake for 20 minutes or until just firm. Cool in the tin.

4   To decorate, preheat the grill. Dissolve 50g (2oz) sugar in a pan with 300ml (½ pint) water. Add the orange zest and simmer for 10–15 minutes until the liquid has reduced and the zest is tender. Drain. Sprinkle the rest of the sugar over the tart. Caramelise under the hot grill, then leave to cool. Spoon the orange zest around the edge to serve.

RASPBERRY AND WHITE CHOCOLATE TARTS

LONG CHILLING REQUIRED

MAKES 8

Preparation: 40 minutes, plus chilling
Cooking time: 40 minutes, plus cooling, chilling
and thawing

225g (8oz) plain flour, plus extra to dust
150g (5oz) butter, cut into cubes
50g (2oz) icing sugar, plus extra to dust
2–3 drops of vanilla extract
1 large egg, lightly beaten
350–450g (12oz–1lb) raspberries
pouring cream to serve

FILLING
275g (10oz) good-quality white chocolate,
    broken into small pieces
300ml (½ pint) double cream
1 vanilla pod, split
2 large eggs, separated
2 tbsp Kirsch

PER TART

648 cals; 49g fat (of which 28g saturates);
52g carbohydrate; 0.6g salt

1 Put the flour, butter and icing sugar into a food processor and pulse until the mixture resembles fine crumbs. (Alternatively, rub the butter into the dry ingredients in a large bowl by hand or using a pastry cutter.) Add the vanilla extract and the beaten egg. Pulse, or stir with a fork, until the dough comes together to form a ball. Wrap in clingfilm and chill for at least 30 minutes.

2 Roll out the pastry thinly on a lightly floured surface. Cut out rounds and use to line eight 9cm (3½ inch), 3cm (1¼ inch) deep, loose-based tart tins. If the pastry cracks as you line the tins, just patch it together. Prick the base all over with a fork, then chill for 30 minutes.

3 Preheat the oven to 200°C (180°C fan oven) mark 6. Bake the pastry cases blind (see page 323). Remove from the oven and leave in the tins to cool slightly. Lower the oven setting to 190°C (170°C fan oven) mark 5.

4 To make the filling, put the chocolate into a bowl. Pour the cream into a small heavy-based pan, add the vanilla and bring just to the boil. Take off the heat and remove the vanilla. Slowly pour the cream on to the chocolate and stir until the chocolate is melted. Leave to cool.

5 Mix the egg yolks and Kirsch into the cooled chocolate mixture. Put the egg whites into a clean, grease-free bowl and whisk until soft peaks form, then fold carefully into the chocolate mixture until evenly incorporated. Pour the filling into the pastry cases.

6 Bake for 10–15 minutes until just set. If the filling appears to be colouring too quickly in the oven, cover with foil. Leave to cool in the tins. Don't worry if the filling seems very soft – it will become firmer on chilling. Chill for at least 5 hours or overnight.

7 Remove from the fridge 30 minutes before serving. Unmould on to plates. Arrange the raspberries on top, dust with icing sugar and serve with cream.

ECCLES CAKES

● ●

MAKES 8–10

Preparation: 10 minutes, plus resting
Cooking time: 15 minutes, plus cooling

212g (7½oz) puff pastry, thawed if frozen
plain flour to dust
25g (1oz) butter, softened
25g (1oz) dark brown soft sugar
25g (1oz) fine chopped mixed peel
50g (2oz) currants
caster sugar to sprinkle

PER CAKE

126–158 calories; 7–9g fat (of which 1–2g saturates); 15–19g carbohydrate; 0.2–0.3g salt

1 Roll out the puff pastry on a lightly floured surface and cut into 9cm (3½ inch) rounds.
2 For the filling, mix the butter, sugar, mixed peel and currants in a bowl.
3 Place 1 tsp of the fruit and butter mixture in the centre of each pastry round. Draw up the edges of each pastry round to enclose the filling, brush the edges with water and pinch together firmly, then reshape. Turn each round over and roll lightly until the currants just show through. Prick the top of each with a fork. Leave to rest for about 10 minutes in a cool place. Preheat the oven to 230°C (210°C fan oven) mark 8.
4 Put the pastry rounds on a damp baking sheet and bake for about 15 minutes until golden. Transfer to a wire rack and leave to cool for 30 minutes. Sprinkle with caster sugar while still warm.

DROP SCONES (SCOTCH PANCAKES)

●●●●●●●●●●●●●●●●●●●●●●●●●●●●●●●●●●●●

MAKES 15–18

Preparation: 10 minutes
Cooking time: 12–18 minutes

125g (4oz) self-raising flour
2 tbsp caster sugar
1 medium egg, beaten
150ml (¼ pint) milk
vegetable oil to grease
butter, or whipped cream and jam, to serve

PER SCONE
50–40 cals; 1g fat (of which 9–7g saturates); 9–7g carbohydrate; 0.1g salt

1 Mix the flour and sugar together in a bowl. Make a well in the centre and mix in
   the egg, with enough of the milk to make a batter the consistency of thick cream –
   working as quickly and lightly as possible.
2 Cook the mixture in batches: drop spoonfuls on to an oiled hot griddle or heavy-
   based frying pan. Keep the griddle at a steady heat and when bubbles rise to the
   surface of the scone and burst, after 2–3 minutes, turn over with a palette knife.
3 Cook for a further 2–3 minutes until golden brown on the other side.
4 Put the cooked drop scones on a clean teatowel and cover with another teatowel
   to keep them moist. Serve warm, with butter, or cream and jam.

WELSH CAKES

● ●

MAKES ABOUT 10

Preparation: 10 minutes
Cooking time: 3 minutes per batch, plus cooling

oil to grease
225g (8oz) plain flour, plus extra to dust
1 tsp baking powder
pinch of salt
50g (2oz) butter or margarine
50g (2oz) lard
75g (3oz) caster sugar
50g (2oz) currants
1 medium egg, beaten
about 2 tbsp milk

PER CAKE

123 calories; 6g fat (of which 3g saturates); 18g carbohydrate; 0.2g salt

1 Lightly oil a griddle or heavy-based frying pan.
2 Sift together the flour, baking powder and salt. Rub in the fats until the mixture resembles fine breadcrumbs. Add the sugar and currants.
3 Make a well in the centre, then add the beaten egg and enough milk to make a stiff paste similar to shortcrust pastry.
4 Roll the paste out on a lightly floured surface until 5mm (¼ inch) thick and then, using a 7.5cm (3 inch) cutter, cut into rounds.
5 Cook the cakes slowly on the griddle for about 3 minutes on each side until golden brown. Cool on a wire rack. Eat on the day they are made.

VARIATION
Griddle scones:
Use the same quantity of self-raising flour (instead of plain flour) with 1 tsp baking powder, pinch of salt and ½ tsp freshly grated nutmeg. Omit the lard. Use 50g (2oz) golden caster sugar. Omit the currants. You may need 3–4 tbsp milk. Roll out to 1cm (½ inch) thick and cut into triangles or rounds. Cook for about 5 minutes on each side. Serve the scones warm, split in half and spread with butter.

BREADS
AND ROLLS

. . . .

WHITE FARMHOUSE LOAF

BREAD MACHINE RECIPE

● ● ● ● ● ● ● ● ● ● ● ● ● ● ● ● ● ●

MAKES 1 LOAF – CUTS INTO ABOUT 12 SLICES

Preparation: 10 minutes, plus kneading

Cooking time: as per your machine, plus cooling

1 tsp easy-blend dried yeast

500g (1lb 2oz) strong white bread flour, plus extra to sprinkle

1 tbsp caster sugar

2 tbsp milk powder

1¹/₂ tsp salt

25g (1oz) butter

350ml (12fl oz) water

PER SLICE

180 cals; 3g fat (of which 1g saturates); 34g carbohydrate; 0.9g salt

1 Put the ingredients into the bread maker bucket, following the order and method specified in the manual.

2 Fit the bucket into the bread maker and set to the Basic programme with a crust of your choice. Press start.

3 Just before baking starts, brush the top of the dough with water and sprinkle with flour. If preferred, slash the top of the bread lengthways with a sharp knife, taking care not to scratch the bucket.

4 After baking, remove the bread from the machine and shake out on to a wire rack to cool.

BROWN LOAF

• •

MAKES 1 LOAF – CUTS INTO 16 SLICES

Preparation: 25 minutes, plus sponging and rising
Cooking time: 45–50 minutes, plus cooling

300g (11oz) strong plain white flour, sifted, plus extra to dust
200g (7oz) strong plain wholemeal flour
15g (½oz) fresh yeast or 1 tsp traditional dried yeast
2 tsp salt
vegetable oil to grease

PER SLICE

100 cals; 1g fat (of which 0.1g saturates); 22g carbohydrate; 0.6g salt

1 Put both flours into a large bowl, make a well in the centre and pour in 300ml (11fl oz) tepid water. Crumble the fresh yeast into the water (if using dried yeast, just sprinkle it over). Draw a little of the flour into the water and yeast and mix to form a batter. Sprinkle the salt over the remaining dry flour, so that it doesn't come into contact with the yeast. Cover with a clean teatowel and leave to 'sponge' for 20 minutes.

2 Combine the flour and salt with the batter to make a soft dough and knead for at least 10 minutes or until the dough feels smooth and elastic. Shape into a ball, put into an oiled bowl, cover with the teatowel and leave to rise at warm room temperature until doubled in size, 2–3 hours.

3 Knock back the dough, knead briefly and shape into a round on a lightly floured baking sheet. Slash the top with a sharp knife and dust with flour. Cover and leave to rise for 45 minutes–1½ hours until doubled in size and spongy.

4 Preheat the oven to 200°C (180°C fan oven) mark 6. Bake the loaf for 45–50 minutes until it sounds hollow when tapped underneath. Transfer to a wire rack and leave to cool.

NOTE

The 'sponging' process in step 1 adds a fermentation stage, which gives a slightly lighter loaf.

WHOLEMEAL BREAD

• •

MAKES 1 LOAF – CUTS INTO 16 SLICES

Preparation: 15 minutes, plus rising
Cooking time: 30–35 minutes, plus cooling

225g (8oz) strong plain white flour, plus extra to dust
450g (1lb) strong plain wholemeal flour
2 tsp salt
1 tsp golden caster sugar
2 tsp fast-action dried yeast (see note)
vegetable oil to grease

PER SLICE

140 cals; 1g fat (of which 0.1g saturates); 29g carbohydrate; 0.6g salt

1 Sift the white flour into a large bowl and stir in the wholemeal flour, salt, sugar and yeast.
Make a well in the centre and add about 450ml (¾ pint) warm water. Work to a
smooth, soft dough, adding a little extra water if necessary.
2 Knead for 10 minutes or until smooth, then shape the dough into a ball and put into
an oiled bowl. Cover and leave to rise in a warm place for about 2 hours until doubled
in size.
3 Knock back the dough on a lightly floured surface and shape into an oblong. Press into
an oiled 900g (2lb) loaf tin, cover and leave to rise for a further 30 minutes.
4 Preheat the oven to 230°C (210°C fan oven) mark 8. Bake the loaf for 15 minutes.
Lower the oven setting to 200°C (180°C fan oven) mark 6 and bake for a further
15–20 minutes until the bread is risen and sounds hollow when tapped underneath.
Leave in the tin for 10 minutes, then turn out on to a wire rack and leave to cool.

NOTE

If available, use 40g (1½oz) fresh yeast instead of dried. Proceed as for White Farmhouse
Loaf (see note, page 214).

DARK RYE BREAD

● ●

MAKES 1 LOAF – CUTS INTO ABOUT 16 SLICES

Preparation: 20 minutes, plus rising
Cooking time: about 50 minutes, plus cooling

350g (12oz) rye flour, plus extra to dust
50g (2oz) plain wholemeal flour
zest of 1 lemon
1 tsp salt
25g (1oz) butter
1 tsp caraway seeds, lightly crushed (optional)
125g (4oz) cool mashed potato
15g (½oz) fresh yeast or 1½ tsp traditional dried yeast and 1 tsp sugar
1 tsp sugar
50g (2oz) molasses or black treacle
oil to grease

PER SLICE

112 calories; 2g fat (of which 1g saturates); 22g carbohydrate; 0.4g salt

1 Mix together the flours, lemon zest and salt. Rub in the butter, caraway seeds, if you like, and mashed potato.

2 Blend the fresh yeast with 150ml (¼ pint) tepid water. If using dried yeast, sprinkle it into the water with 1 tsp sugar and leave in a warm place for 15 minutes or until frothy. Heat the other 1 tsp sugar, molasses and 2 tbsp water together. Cool until tepid.

3 Pour the yeast liquid and molasses mixture on to the dry ingredients and beat well to form a firm dough. Knead on a lightly floured surface for 10 minutes or until smooth and no longer sticky. Place in an oiled bowl, cover with oiled clingfilm and leave to rise in a warm place for about 1½ hours until doubled in size.

4 Knead again for 5 minutes, then shape into a large round, about 18cm (7 inch) in diameter. Place on a baking sheet. Cut a criss-cross pattern on the surface of the loaf to a depth of 5mm (¼ inch). Dust with a little more flour. Leave to rise in a warm place for 10–15 minutes. Preheat the oven to 200°C (180°C fan oven) mark 6.

5 Bake the loaf in the oven for about 50 minutes. Turn out on to a wire rack and leave to cool completely.

FREEZING TIP
To freeze, complete the recipe. Once the bread is cold, slice, if you like, for convenience, then pack, seal and freeze. To use, thaw at cool room temperature.

OATMEAL SODA BREAD

MAKES I LOAF – CUTS INTO ABOUT 10 SLICES

Preparation: 15 minutes
Cooking time: 25 minutes, plus cooling

25g (1oz) butter, plus extra to grease
275g (10oz) plain wholemeal flour
175g (6oz) coarse oatmeal
2 tsp cream of tartar
1 tsp salt
about 300ml (10fl oz) milk and water, mixed

PER SLICE

183 cals; 4g fat (of which 2g saturates); 31g carbohydrate; 0.6g salt

1 Preheat the oven to 220°C (200°C fan oven) mark 7. Grease
   and base-line a 900g (2lb) loaf tin.
2 Mix together all the dry ingredients in a bowl. Rub in the
   butter, then add the milk and water to bind to a soft dough.
   Spoon into the prepared tin.
3 Bake in the oven for about 25 minutes until golden brown and
   well risen. Turn out on to a wire rack and leave to cool slightly.
   It is best eaten on the day it is made.

CORNBREAD

● ● ● ● ● ● ● ● ● ● ● ● ● ● ● ● ● ● ● ●

SERVES 8

Preparation: 5 minutes
Cooking time: 25–30 minutes

oil to grease
125g (4oz) plain flour
175g (6oz) polenta (see note) or cornmeal
1 tbsp baking powder
1 tbsp caster sugar
½ tsp salt
300ml (½ pint) buttermilk, or equal quantities of natural yogurt and
    milk, mixed together
2 medium eggs
4 tbsp extra virgin olive oil

PER SERVING

229 cals; 8g fat (of which 1g saturates); 33g carbohydrate; 1.3g salt

1 Preheat the oven to 200°C (180°C fan oven) mark 6.
   Generously oil a 20.5cm (8 inch) square shallow tin.
2 Put the flour into a large bowl, then add the polenta or
   cornmeal, the baking powder, sugar and salt. Make a well in the
   centre and pour in the buttermilk or yogurt and milk mixture.
   Add the eggs and olive oil and stir together until evenly mixed.
3 Pour into the tin and bake for 25–30 minutes until firm to the
   touch. Insert a skewer into the centre – if it comes out clean,
   the cornbread is done.
4 Leave the cornbread to rest in the tin for 5 minutes, then turn
   out and cut into chunky triangles. Serve warm with butter.

NOTE
Use dried polenta grains for this recipe.

FLOURY BAPS

●●●

MAKES 8 BAPS

Preparation: 10 minutes, plus kneading and rising
Cooking time: 18–20 minutes, plus cooling

1 tsp easy-blend dried yeast
450g (1lb) strong white bread flour, plus extra to dust
1 tsp salt
1 tsp golden caster sugar
15g (½oz) butter
150ml (¼ pint) milk, plus extra to brush
oil to grease

PER BAP
220 cals; 3g fat (of which 1g saturates); 45g carbohydrate; 0.7g salt

1 Put all the ingredients except the oil into the bread maker bucket with 125ml (4fl oz) water, following the order and method specified in the manual.

2 Fit the bucket into the bread maker and set to the dough programme. Press start. Lightly oil a large baking sheet.

3 Once the dough is ready, turn it out on to a lightly floured surface and punch it down to deflate. Divide into 8 even-sized pieces. Shape each piece into a round and flatten with the palm of your hand until about 10cm (4 inch) in diameter.

4 Space slightly apart on the baking sheet and brush lightly with milk. Sprinkle generously with flour, cover loosely with a cloth and leave to rise for 30–40 minutes until doubled in size.

5 Preheat the oven to 200°C (180°C fan oven) mark 6. Using your thumb, make a deep impression in the centre of each bap. Dust with a little more flour and bake for 18–20 minutes until risen and pale golden around the edges. Eat warm or transfer to a wire rack to cool.

CRUMPETS

• •

MAKES ABOUT 24

Preparation: 20 minutes, plus rising
Cooking time: about 35 minutes

350g (12oz) strong plain white flour
½ tsp salt
½ tsp bicarbonate of soda
1½ tsp fast-action dried yeast
250ml (9fl oz) warm milk
a little vegetable oil to fry
butter to serve

PER CRUMPET

60 cals; 1g fat (of which 0.1g saturates); 12g carbohydrate; 0.2g salt

1 Sift the flour, salt and bicarbonate of soda into a large bowl and stir in the yeast. Make a well in the centre, then pour in 300ml (½ pint) warm water and the milk. Mix to a thick batter.

2 Using a wooden spoon, beat the batter vigorously for about 5 minutes. Cover and leave in a warm place for about 1 hour until sponge-like in texture. Beat the batter for a further 2 minutes, then transfer to a jug.

3 Put a large non-stick frying pan over a high heat and brush a little oil over the surface. Oil the insides of four crumpet rings or 7.5cm (3 inch) plain metal cutters. Put the rings, blunt-edge down, on to the hot pan surface and leave for about 2 minutes until very hot.

4 Pour a little batter into each ring to a depth of 1cm (½ inch). Cook the crumpets for 4–5 minutes until the surface is set and appears honeycombed with holes.

5 Carefully remove each metal ring. Flip the crumpets over and cook the other side for 1 minute only. Transfer to a wire rack. Repeat to use all of the batter.

6 To serve, toast the crumpets on both sides and serve with butter.

NOTE
The pan and metal rings must be well oiled each time, and heated between frying each batch.

PARMESAN AND OLIVE GRISSINI

MAKES 32

Preparation: 20 minutes, plus kneading and rising
Cooking time: 18–20 minutes, plus cooling

1 tsp easy-blend dried yeast
500g (1lb 2oz) strong white bread flour
1 tsp salt
3 tbsp olive oil
2 tsp golden caster sugar
300ml (½ pint) water
50g (2oz) pitted black olives, finely chopped
50g (2oz) Parmesan, freshly grated

TO FINISH
oil to grease
semolina to dust
beaten egg to glaze
coarse salt flakes to sprinkle

PER GRISSINI
872 cals; 2g fat (of which 0.5g saturates); 12g carbohydrate; 0.3g salt

1 Put all the dough ingredients except the olives and Parmesan into the bread maker bucket with 300ml (½ pint) water, following the order and method specified in the manual.

2 Fit the bucket into the bread maker and set to the dough programme with raisin setting, if available. Press start. Add the olives and Parmesan when the machine beeps, or halfway through the kneading cycle. Lightly oil two large baking sheets and sprinkle with semolina.

3 Once the dough is ready, turn out on to a surface and punch it down to deflate. Cover with a teatowel and leave to rest for 10 minutes.

4 Roll out the dough to a 30.5 × 20.5cm (12 × 8 inch) rectangle, cover loosely with a teatowel and leave for 30 minutes until well risen.

5 Preheat the oven to 220°C (fan oven 200°C) mark 7. Cut the dough across the width into 4 thick bands. From each of these, cut 8 very thin strips and transfer them to the baking sheet, stretching each one until it is about 28cm (11 inch) long, and spacing the strips 1cm (½ inch) apart.

6 Brush very lightly with beaten egg and sprinkle with salt flakes. Bake for 18–20 minutes until crisp and golden. Transfer to a wire rack to cool.

NOTE
For convenience, make them several days in advance and store in an airtight tin. To serve, pop them into a moderate oven for a couple of minutes if they have softened slightly.

ROASTED RED ONION AND GRUYÈRE BREAD

BREAD MACHINE RECIPE

**MAKES I ROUND BREAD – CUTS INTO
6 LARGE WEDGES**

Preparation: 20 minutes, plus kneading and rising

Cooking time: 25–30 minutes

2 tsp fennel seeds
I tsp easy-blend dried yeast
300g (11oz) strong white bread flour, plus extra to dust
½ tsp celery salt
I tsp golden caster sugar
2 tbsp olive oil

TOPPING
3 tbsp olive oil, plus extra to grease
450g (1lb) red onions, peeled and thinly sliced
several fresh thyme sprigs, chopped
100g (3½oz) Gruyère cheese, thinly sliced
salt and ground black pepper

PER WEDGE
348 cals; 16g fat (of which 5g saturates); 44g carbohydrate; 0.7g salt

1 Lightly crush the fennel seeds, using a pestle and mortar. Put all the dough ingredients into the bread maker bucket with 200ml (7fl oz) water, following the order and method specified in the manual, adding the crushed fennel seeds with the flour.

2 Fit the bucket into the bread maker and set to the dough programme with pizza setting, if available, if not then the dough setting. Press start.

3 While the dough is in the bread maker, prepare the topping. Heat the oil in a frying pan, add the onions and fry gently for about 10 minutes until golden, stirring frequently. Stir in the thyme and seasoning.

4 Place a 28cm (11 inch) round metal flan ring on a baking sheet (see note). Brush the inside of the ring and baking sheet with oil.

5 Once the dough is ready, turn it out on to a floured surface, knead lightly and roll out to a 28cm (11 inch) round. Lift the dough round into the ring on the baking sheet. Arrange the fried onion and cheese slices over the surface to within 1cm (½ inch) of the edges. Cover loosely with oiled clingfilm and leave in a warm place for 20 minutes. Preheat the oven to 220°C (fan oven 200°C) mark 7.

6 Bake for 25–30 minutes until the crust is slightly risen and golden. Serve warm, cut into wedges.

NOTE
If you do not have a suitably sized metal flan ring, simply roll the dough to a large round and place directly on the baking sheet.

SWEET CHERRY BREAD

CUTS INTO 8 SLICES

Preparation: 40 minutes, plus rising
Cooking time: 40 minutes, plus cooling

oil to grease
350g (12oz) strong white bread flour, plus extra to dust
½ tsp salt
2 tsp ground mixed spice
1 tsp ground cinnamon
25g (1oz) caster sugar
1 tbsp fast-action dried yeast
75g (3oz) unsalted butter, diced
200ml (7fl oz) warm milk
125g (4oz) white almond paste, roughly chopped
125g (4oz) glacé cherries
3 tbsp honey, warmed
75g (3oz) icing sugar, sifted

PER SLICE

310 cals; 4g fat (of which trace saturates); 66g carbohydrate; 0.4g salt

1 Grease a 20.5cm (8 inch) round deep cake tin and base-line with greaseproof paper.
2 Sift the flour, salt, spices and caster sugar into a bowl. Add the yeast, then rub in the butter. Add the milk to make a dough (if the dough is too dry, add a little more milk). Turn out on to a lightly floured surface and knead for 10 minutes. Put the dough into a lightly oiled bowl, cover with oiled clingfilm and leave in a warm place for 2 hours or until doubled in size.
3 Turn out the dough on to a lightly floured surface and knead lightly. Shape into an oval, 60cm (24 inch) long. Scatter the almond paste and cherries over the surface and roll up the dough lengthways, then form it into a tight coil. Put in the cake tin, cover and leave in a warm place for 30 minutes or until doubled in size. Preheat the oven to 180°C (160°C fan oven) mark 4.
4 Bake for 40 minutes or until golden; it should sound hollow when tapped underneath. Turn out on to a wire rack and leave to cool completely. When cool, brush with honey. Mix the icing sugar with a few drops of water and drizzle over the bread.

TO STORE
Store in an airtight container. It will keep for up to two days.

APRICOT AND HAZELNUT BREAD

●●●●●●●●●●●●●●●●●●●●●●●

MAKES 2 LOAVES – EACH CUTS INTO ABOUT 10 SLICES

Preparation: 25 minutes, plus rising

Cooking time: 30–35 minutes, plus cooling

75g (3oz) hazelnuts
450g (1lb) strong Granary bread flour, plus extra to dust
1 tsp salt
25g (1oz) unsalted butter, diced
75g (3oz) ready-to-eat dried apricots, chopped
2 tsp fast-action dried yeast
2 tbsp molasses
oil to grease
milk to glaze

PER SLICE

118 cals; 4g fat (of which 0.9g saturates); 18g carbohydrate; 0.3g salt

1 Spread the hazelnuts on a baking sheet. Toast under a hot grill until golden brown, turning frequently. Put the hazelnuts in a clean teatowel and rub off the skins. Leave to cool. Chop and put to one side.

2 Put the flour into a large bowl. Add the salt, then rub in the butter. Stir in the hazelnuts, apricots and yeast. Make a well in the centre and gradually work in the molasses and about 225ml (8fl oz) hand-hot water to form a soft dough, adding a little more water if the dough feels dry. Knead for 8–10 minutes until smooth, then transfer the dough to an oiled bowl, cover and leave to rise in a warm place for 1–1¼ hours until doubled in size.

3 Punch the dough to knock back, then divide in half. Shape each portion into a small, flattish round and put on a well-floured baking sheet. Cover loosely and leave to rise for a further 30 minutes.

4 Preheat the oven to 220°C (200°C fan oven) mark 7 and put a large baking sheet on the top shelf to heat up.

5 Using a sharp knife, cut several slashes on each round, brush with a little milk and transfer to the heated baking sheet. Bake for 15 minutes, then lower the oven setting to 190°C (170°C fan oven) mark 5 and bake for a further 15–20 minutes until the bread is risen and sounds hollow when tapped underneath. Turn out on to a wire rack and leave to cool completely.

TO STORE

Store in an airtight container. It will keep for up to two days.

VARIATION

Replace the hazelnuts with walnuts or pecan nuts and use sultanas instead of apricots.

FRUITED MUESLI LOAF

**MAKES I MEDIUM LOAF – CUTS INTO ABOUT
10 SLICES**

Preparation: 10 minutes, plus kneading
Cooking time: as per your machine, plus cooling

1 ½ tsp easy-blend dried yeast
225g (8oz) strong white bread flour
100g (3½oz) strong brown bread flour
100g (3½oz) natural (no added sugar or salt) muesli
1 tsp salt
1 tbsp clear honey, plus 2 tbsp clear honey to glaze
50g (2oz) raisins
25g (1oz) butter

PER SLICE
200 cals; 3g fat (of which 2g saturates); 39g carbohydrate; 0.6g salt

1 Put all the ingredients except the honey to glaze into the bread maker bucket with 250ml (9fl oz) water, following the order and method specified in the manual.
2 Fit the bucket into the bread maker and set to the programme recommended in the manual, usually multigrain. Select the crust of your choice and press start.
3 After baking, remove the bucket from the machine, then turn out the loaf on to a wire rack to cool. Brush the top of the loaf with honey to glaze.

FREEZING TIP
To freeze, complete the recipe. Once the bread is cold, slice, if you like, for convenience, then pack, seal and freeze. To use, thaw at cool room temperature.

CHOCOLATE MACADAMIA LOAF

BREAD MACHINE RECIPE

MAKES I MEDIUM LOAF – CUTS INTO ABOUT 10 SLICES

Preparation: 15 minutes, plus kneading

Cooking time: 15 minutes, plus baking time as per your machine and cooling and setting

100g (3½oz) macadamia nuts, roughly chopped
1 large egg, plus 2 egg yolks
75g (3oz) unsalted butter, melted
2 tsp finely chopped fresh rosemary
1¼ tsp easy-blend dried yeast
400g (14oz) strong white bread flour
¾ tsp salt
50g (2oz) golden caster sugar
75g (3oz) plain chocolate, chopped
175g (6oz) white chocolate, chopped

PER SLICE

450 cals; 25g fat (of which 10g saturates); 52g carbohydrate; 0.6g salt

1 Lightly toast the nuts in a frying pan over a low heat for about 3 minutes, shaking the pan frequently. Tip on to a plate and set aside.

2 Mix together the egg, egg yolks, butter, rosemary and 175ml (6fl oz) water. Put all the ingredients except the nuts and chocolate into the bread maker bucket, following the order and method specified in the manual.

3 Fit the bucket into the bread maker and set to the basic programme with raisin setting, if available. Select a light crust and press start. Add the nuts, plain chocolate and 125g (4oz) white chocolate when the machine beeps, or halfway through the kneading programme.

4 After baking, remove the bucket from the machine, then turn out the bread on to a wire rack to cool. Once the bread has cooled, melt the remaining white chocolate carefully in a heatproof bowl set over a pan of hot water, making sure the base of the bowl doesn't touch the water. Stir until smooth, then spread over the top of the loaf. Leave to set.

NOTE
Macadamia nuts are mildly flavoured with an almost buttery taste – not a coincidence, as the nut has a high oil content.

STICKY CURRANT BUNS

BREAD MACHINE RECIPE

MAKES 8

Preparation: 10 minutes, plus kneading and rising

Cooking time: 10–15 minutes, plus cooling

1 tsp easy-blend dried yeast
350g (12oz) strong white bread flour, plus extra to dust
½ tsp salt
1 tsp ground mixed spice
15g (½oz) butter, plus extra to grease
finely grated zest of 1 orange
25g (1oz) light muscovado sugar
200ml (7fl oz) milk
75g (3oz) currants
oil to grease

TO FINISH

25g (1oz) light muscovado sugar
50g (2oz) rough sugar pieces, lightly crushed

PER BUN

250 cals; 3g fat (of which 1g saturates); 53g carbohydrate; 0.4g salt

1 Put all the dough ingredients except the currants and oil into the bread maker bucket, following the order and method specified in the manual.
2 Fit the bucket into the bread maker and set to the dough programme with raisin setting, if available. Add the currants when the machine beeps, or halfway through the kneading cycle. Lightly grease a large baking sheet.
3 Once the dough is ready, turn out on to a floured surface and punch it down to deflate. Divide into 8 evenly sized pieces, scrunch into rounds and space slightly apart on the baking sheet. Cover with oiled clingfilm and leave to rise in a warm place for 30 minutes until doubled in size. Preheat the oven to 220°C (200°C fan oven) mark 7.
4 Bake the buns for 10–15 minutes until golden. Meanwhile, put the muscovado sugar in a small pan with 2 tbsp water and heat gently until the sugar dissolves.
5 Transfer the buns to a wire rack and brush with the glaze, sprinkling them with the crushed sugar as you work. Leave to cool.

NOTE

It's the rough, craggy appearance of these buns that makes them so inviting, so don't waste time rolling and shaping them carefully.

PANETTONE

● ●

CUTS INTO ABOUT 10 SLICES

Preparation: 20 minutes, plus standing
Cooking time: 1 hour

450g (1lb) plain white flour
20g (¾oz) fresh yeast or 2¼ tsp traditional dried yeast
225ml (8fl oz) tepid milk
125g (4oz) butter, softened, plus extra to grease
2 medium egg yolks
50g (2oz) caster sugar
75g (3oz) chopped mixed candied peel
50g (2oz) sultanas
pinch of freshly grated nutmeg
egg yolk to glaze

PER SLICE
285 calories; 12g fat (of which 7g saturates); 41g carbohydrate; 0.3g salt

1 Sift the flour into a large bowl and make a well in the centre. Blend the fresh yeast with the milk. If using dried yeast, sprinkle it on to the milk and leave in a warm place for 15 minutes or until frothy. Add the yeast liquid to the flour and mix well together, gradually drawing in the flour from the sides of the bowl. Leave to stand in a warm place for 45 minutes or until doubled in size.

2 Add the softened butter to the dough with the 2 egg yolks, the sugar, candied peel, sultanas and nutmeg. Mix well. Leave to stand again in a warm place for a further 45 minutes or until doubled in size.

3 Meanwhile, line an 18cm (7 inch) circular tin with baking parchment. Place the dough inside the tin and leave in a warm place for about 1 hour until risen to the top. Preheat the oven to 200°C (180°C fan oven) mark 6.

4 Brush the top of the dough with egg yolk to glaze. Bake on the lowest shelf of the oven for 20 minutes, then lower the oven setting to 180°C (160°C fan oven) mark 4 and cook for a further 40 minutes or until a fine warmed skewer inserted into the centre comes out clean. Leave to cool in the tin.

TO STORE
Store in an airtight container. It will keep for up to one week.

LEMON-GLAZED CHELSEA BUNS

BREAD MACHINE RECIPE

MAKES 12

Preparation: 15 minutes, plus kneading and rising
Cooking time: 25–30 minutes, plus cooling

1 large egg
50g (2oz) unsalted butter, melted, plus extra to grease
225ml (8fl oz) milk
1½ tsp easy-blend dried yeast
400g (14oz) strong white bread flour, plus extra to dust
100g (3½oz) strong soft grain or Granary flour
1 tsp salt
75g (3oz) light muscovado sugar

FILLING AND TOPPING

2 pieces preserved stem ginger, plus 3 tbsp syrup
100g (3½oz) raisins
100g (3½oz) sultanas
50g (2oz) light muscovado sugar
2 tsp ground mixed spice
finely grated zest and juice of 1 lemon
40g (1½oz) unsalted butter, cut into pieces

PER BUN

310 cals; 8g fat (of which 4g saturates); 56g carbohydrate; 0.6g salt

1 In a bowl, whisk the egg, butter and milk together with a fork. Put all the dough ingredients into the bread maker bucket, following the order and method specified in the manual.
2 Fit the bucket into the bread maker and set to the dough programme. Press start.
3 Grease a 23cm (9 inch) square cake tin, 7.5cm (3 inch) deep. For the filling, finely chop the stem ginger and mix in a bowl with the raisins, sultanas, 25g (1oz) sugar, the spice and lemon zest.
4 Once the dough is ready, turn out on to a floured surface and punch it down to deflate. Roll out to a 30.5cm (12 inch) square and spread with the filling to within 1cm (½ inch) of the edges. Dot with the butter. Roll up the dough to enclose the filling, then cut into 2.5cm (1 inch) thick slices.

5 Pack the slices, cut-sides uppermost, into the prepared tin, spacing them evenly apart. Cover with oiled clingfilm and leave to rise in a warm place for about 45 minutes until doubled in size and rising up towards the top of the tin. Preheat the oven to 200°C (180°C fan oven) mark 6.
6 Bake the buns for 20 minutes, then lower the oven setting to 180°C (160°C fan oven) mark 4 and bake for a further 5–10 minutes until risen and deep golden. In the meantime, mix together the remaining sugar, lemon juice and stem ginger syrup to make a glaze. Transfer the buns to a wire rack and brush with the glaze. Leave to cool until warm.

NOTE

Like most fruity breads, these are best eaten warm, so if you make them ahead, pop them in the oven for a few minutes before serving.

PISTACHIO AND ROSEWATER STOLLEN

BREAD MACHINE RECIPE

● ● ● ● ● ● ● ● ● ● ● ● ● ● ● ● ●

MAKES 1 STOLLEN – CUTS INTO ABOUT 10 THICK SLICES

Preparation: 15 minutes, plus kneading and rising
Cooking time: 20–25 minutes, plus cooling

1¼ tsp easy-blend dried yeast
350g (12oz) strong white bread flour, plus extra to dust
½ tsp salt
1 tsp ground mixed spice
25g (1oz) golden caster sugar
50g (2oz) butter, melted
150ml (¼ pint) milk
3 tbsp rosewater
75g (3oz) sultanas
50g (2oz) pistachio nuts
50g (2oz) chopped mixed candied peel
icing sugar to dust

MARZIPAN

150g (5oz) pistachio nuts, skinned (see note)
40g (1½oz) golden caster sugar
40g (1½oz) golden icing sugar
2 medium egg yolks
oil to grease

PER SLICE

380 cals; 17g fat (of which 5g saturates); 51g carbohydrate; 0.7g salt

1 Put all the dough ingredients except the sultanas, pistachio nuts, candied peel and icing sugar into the bread maker bucket, following the order and method specified in the manual.

2 Fit the bucket into the bread maker and set to the dough programme with raisin setting, if available. Press start. Add the sultanas, pistachio nuts and candied peel when the machine beeps, or halfway through the kneading cycle.

3 Meanwhile, make the marzipan. Put the pistachio nuts in a food processor and blend until finely ground. Add the sugars and egg yolks and blend to a paste. Turn out on to the worksurface and shape into a log, 24cm (9½ inch) long. Grease a large baking sheet.

4 Once the dough is ready, turn out on to a floured surface and punch it down to deflate. Roll out to an oblong, 28cm (11 inch) long and 15cm (6 inch) wide. Lay the marzipan on the dough, slightly to one side of the centre. Brush the long edges of the dough with water, then fold the wider piece of dough over the paste, sealing well.

5 Transfer to the baking sheet, cover loosely with oiled clingfilm and leave in a warm place for about 40 minutes until doubled in size. Preheat the oven to 200°C (180°C fan oven) mark 6.

6 Bake for 20–25 minutes until risen and golden. Transfer to a wire rack to cool. Serve lavishly dusted with icing sugar.

NOTE

For a vibrantly coloured marzipan it's best to skin the pistachios first – soak them in boiling water for a couple of minutes, then rub between pieces of kitchen paper to remove the skins.

CROISSANTS

● ●

MAKES 12

Preparation: 40 minutes, plus chilling and standing
Cooking time: 15 minutes

25g (1oz) fresh yeast or 1 tbsp dried yeast and 1 tsp sugar
2 medium eggs
450g (1lb) strong white flour, plus extra to dust
2 tsp salt
25g (1oz) lard
225g (8oz) unsalted butter, at cool room temperature
½ tsp caster sugar

PER CROISSANT
300 cals; 19g fat (of which 11g saturates); 29g carbohydrate; 1.1g salt

1 Blend the fresh yeast with 225ml (8fl oz) tepid water. If using dried yeast, sprinkle it
   into the water with the sugar and leave in a warm place for 15 minutes or until frothy.
2 Whisk 1 egg into the yeast liquid. Sift the flour and salt into a large bowl and rub in
   the lard. Make a well in the centre and pour in the yeast liquid. Mix and then beat in
   the flour until the bowl is left clean. Turn out on to a lightly floured surface and knead
   well for about 10 minutes until the dough is firm and elastic.
3 Roll out the dough on a lightly floured surface to an oblong about 51 × 20.5cm
   (20 × 8 inch). Keep the edges as square as possible, gently pulling out the corners
   to stop them rounding off. Dust the rolling pin with flour to prevent it sticking to
   the dough.
4 Divide the butter into three. Dot one portion over the top two-thirds of the dough
   but clear of the edge. Turn up the bottom third of the dough over half the butter, then
   fold down the remainder. Seal the edges with a rolling pin. Turn the dough so that the
   fold is on the right.
5 Press the dough lightly at intervals along its length, then roll out to an oblong again.
   Repeat the rolling and folding with the other two portions of butter. Rest the dough
   in the fridge for 30 minutes, loosely covered with a clean teatowel. Repeat three more
   times, cover and chill for 1 hour.
6 Roll out the dough to an oblong about 48 × 33cm (19 × 13 inch), lay a clean teatowel
   over the top and leave to rest for 10 minutes. Trim off 1cm (½ inch) all around and
   divide the dough in half lengthways, then into three squares, then across into triangles.
7 Beat the remaining egg, 1 tbsp water and the sugar together for the glaze and brush
   it over the triangles. Roll each triangle up from the long edge, finishing with the tip
   underneath. Curve into crescents and place well apart on ungreased baking sheets,
   allowing room to spread. Cover loosely with a clean teatowel. Leave at room
   temperature for about 30 minutes until well risen and 'puffy'.
8 Preheat the oven to 220°C (200°C fan oven) mark 7. Brush each croissant carefully
   with more glaze. Bake in the oven for 15 minutes or until crisp and well browned.

DANISH PASTRIES

● ●

MAKES 16

Preparation: 20 minutes, plus resting and rising
Cooking time: 15 minutes

25g (1oz) fresh yeast or 1 tbsp traditional
 dried yeast and 1 tsp sugar
450g (1lb) plain white flour, plus extra to
 dust
1 tsp salt
50g (2oz) lard
2 tbsp caster sugar
2 medium eggs, beaten
300g (10oz) butter or margarine, softened
beaten egg to glaze
glacé icing (see page 312) and flaked
 almonds to decorate

ALMOND PASTE
15g (½oz) butter or margarine
75g (3oz) caster sugar
75g (3oz) ground almonds
1 medium egg, beaten

CINNAMON BUTTER
50g (2oz) butter
50g (2oz) caster sugar
2 tsp ground cinnamon

PER DANISH
376 cals; 25g fat (of which 14g saturates);
35g carbohydrate; 0.7g salt

1 Blend the fresh yeast with 150ml (¼ pint) tepid water. If using dried yeast, sprinkle it into the water with the 1 tsp sugar and leave in a warm place for 15 minutes or until frothy.
2 Mix the flour and salt, rub in the lard and stir in the 2 tbsp sugar. Add the yeast liquid and beaten eggs and mix to an elastic dough, adding a little more water if necessary. Knead well for 5 minutes on a lightly floured surface until smooth. Return the dough to the rinsed-out bowl, cover with a clean teatowel and leave the dough to rest in the fridge for 10 minutes.
3 Shape the butter or margarine into an oblong. Roll out the dough on a lightly floured surface to an oblong about three times as wide as the butter. Put the butter in the centre of the dough and fold the sides of the dough over the butter. Press the edges to seal.
4 With the folds at the sides, roll the dough into a strip three times as long as it is wide; fold the bottom third up and the top third down, cover and rest for 10 minutes. Turn, repeat, rolling, folding and resting twice more.
5 To make the almond paste, cream the butter or margarine and sugar, stir in the almonds and add enough egg to make a soft and pliable consistency.
6 Make the cinnamon butter by creaming the butter and sugar and beating in the cinnamon.
7 Roll out the dough into the required shapes (see right) and fill with almond paste or cinnamon butter.
8 After shaping, cover the pastries with a clean teatowel and leave to prove in a warm place for 20–30 minutes. Preheat the oven to 220°C (200°C fan oven) mark 7. Brush the pastries with beaten egg and bake for 15 minutes. While hot, brush with thin glacé icing and sprinkle with flaked almonds.

SHAPING DANISH PASTRIES
Imperial stars:
Cut into 7.5cm (3 inch) squares and make diagonal cuts from each corner to within 1cm (½ inch) of the centre. Put a piece of almond paste in the centre of the square and fold one corner of each cut section down to the centre, securing the tips with beaten egg.

Foldovers and cushions:
Cut into 7.5cm (3 inch) squares and put a little almond paste in the centre. Fold over two opposite corners to the centre. Make a cushion by folding over all four corners. Secure the tips with a little beaten egg.

Twists:
Cut into 25.5 x 10cm (10 x 4 inch) rectangles. Cut each rectangle lengthways to give four pieces. Spread with cinnamon butter and fold the bottom third of each up and the top third down, seal and cut each across into thin slices. Twist these slices and put on a baking sheet.

STRAWBERRY DOUGHNUTS

• •

MAKES 12

Preparation: 25 minutes, plus rising
Cooking time: about 20 minutes

250g (9oz) plain flour, plus extra to dust
1 x 7g sachet fast-action yeast
100g (3½oz) caster sugar
100ml (3½fl oz) milk
25g (1oz) butter
1 medium egg
sunflower oil to deep-fry
175g (6oz) 'no bits' strawberry jam
½ tsp ground cinnamon

PER DOUGHNUT

261 cals; 13g fat (of which 3g saturates); 35g carbohydrate; 0.1g salt

1   Put the flour, yeast and half the sugar into a large bowl. Heat the milk and butter in a small pan until just warm. Tip into a jug and beat in the egg. Working quickly, pour the liquid into the flour mixture and stir to make a soft dough. Tip on to a lightly floured surface and knead for 5 minutes or until smooth and elastic. Return the dough to the bowl, cover with clingfilm and leave to rise in a warm place for 30–40 minutes.

2   Line a baking sheet with parchment paper. When the dough is ready, tip on to a lightly floured surface. Gently pat out into a rough rectangle 1cm (½ inch) thick and, using a 5.5cm (2¼ inch) round pastry cutter, stamp out 12 rounds. Transfer to the baking sheet, cover loosely with clingfilm and leave to rise in a warm place for 20 minutes.

3   Fill a large saucepan one-third full with oil and heat to 150°C, using a thermometer. Fry the doughnuts in batches of four until deep golden brown, about 7 minutes, turning over halfway through the cooking time. Using a slotted spoon, lift the doughnuts on to kitchen paper to drain and leave to cool for 5 minutes. Cook the remaining doughnuts in the same way.

4   Fit a piping bag with a 5mm (¼ inch) plain nozzle and fill with the jam. Use a skewer to poke a hole into the centre of each doughnut through the side, then push the piping nozzle in and squirt in some jam. Mix the remaining caster sugar with the cinnamon and tip on to a plate. Roll the filled doughnuts in the sugar mixture and serve warm.

NOTE
To oven-bake your doughnuts, complete the recipe to the end of step 2. Next, preheat the oven to 200°C (180°C fan oven) mark 6 and bake the doughnuts for 15 minutes or until puffed and golden. Complete the recipe from step 4, brushing the doughnuts with oil before coating in the sugar mixture.

KUGELHOPF

OVERNIGHT CHILLING REQUIRED

CUTS INTO 12 SLICES

Preparation: 45 minutes, plus soaking, chilling and rising
Cooking time: 50–55 minutes, plus cooling

200g (7oz) raisins, black seedless if possible
3 tbsp light rum
2 tsp fast-action dried yeast
300g (11oz) plain white flour, plus extra to dust
4 large eggs
100ml (3½fl oz) milk
225g (8oz) unsalted butter, softened, plus extra to grease
75g (3oz) caster sugar
pinch of salt
zest of 1 lemon
100g (3½oz) split blanched almonds, lightly toasted
whole glacé fruits and nuts to decorate
icing sugar to dust

PER SLICE

382 cals; 22g fat (of which 11g saturates); 39g carbohydrate; 0.4g salt

1 Combine the raisins and rum, cover and soak overnight. Put the yeast and flour into a food mixer. Lightly whisk the eggs and milk and then, with the machine running on a slow speed, pour in the egg mixture and mix for 10 minutes or until the dough is very smooth, shiny and elastic. In another bowl, beat the butter, caster sugar, salt and lemon zest and then, with the mixer running, add to the dough, a spoonful at a time, until evenly incorporated. Turn the mixture into a large, lightly floured bowl. Cover with clingfilm and chill overnight.

2 Generously butter a 2 litre (3½ pint) kugelhopf ring mould. Press one-third of the almonds on to the sides of the mould. Chill. Roughly chop the remaining almonds. Mix by hand into the dough with the raisins and rum, then put into the mould, cover and leave for 3 hours in a warm place until it feels spongy and has risen to within 2cm (¾ inch) of the top of the mould.

3 Preheat the oven to 200°C (180°C fan oven) mark 6. Bake the kugelhopf on a shelf below the centre of the oven for 10 minutes. Cover with greaseproof paper, lower the oven setting to 190°C (170°C fan oven) mark 5 and bake for 40–45 minutes until the kugelhopf sounds hollow when you tap the mould. Cool in the tin for 15 minutes, then turn out on to a wire rack and leave to cool completely. Decorate with glacé fruits and nuts and serve dusted with icing sugar.

NOTES

- If you don't have a mixer with a beater attachment, use a food processor with a flat plastic blade.
- This cake is made with yeast, so it's best eaten within two days or it will go stale. If you have any left over, wrap and freeze in slices – toast or use for making bread and butter pudding.

BRIOCHE

SERVES 10

Preparation: 20 minutes, plus rising
Cooking time: 15–20 minutes, plus cooling

15g (½oz) fresh yeast or 1½ tsp fast-action dried yeast
225g (8oz) strong plain white flour, plus extra to dust
pinch of salt
1 tbsp golden caster sugar
2 extra large eggs, beaten
50g (2oz) butter, melted and cooled until tepid
vegetable oil to grease
beaten egg to glaze

PER SERVING
140 cals; 6g fat (of which 3g saturates); 19g carbohydrate; 0.2g salt

1 If using fresh yeast, blend with 2 tbsp tepid water. Mix the flour, salt and sugar together in a large bowl. (Stir in fast-action dried yeast if using.)
2 Make a well in the centre and pour in the yeast liquid (or 2 tbsp tepid water if using fast-action dried yeast) plus the eggs and melted butter. Work the ingredients together to a soft dough.
3 Turn out on to a lightly floured surface and knead for about 5 minutes until smooth and elastic. Put the dough into a large oiled bowl, cover and leave in a warm place for about 1 hour until doubled in size.
4 Knock back the dough on a lightly floured surface. Shape three-quarters of it into a ball and put into an oiled 1.2 litre (2 pint) brioche mould. Press a hole through the centre. Shape the remaining dough into a round, put on top of the brioche and press down lightly. Cover and leave in a warm place until the dough is puffy and nearly risen to the top of the mould.
5 Preheat the oven to 230°C (210°C fan oven) mark 8. Brush the brioche dough lightly with beaten egg and bake for 15–20 minutes until golden.
6 Turn out on to a wire rack and leave to cool. Serve warm or cold.

NOTE
For individual brioches, divide the dough into 10 pieces. Shape as above. Bake in individual tins, for 10 minutes.

HOT CROSS BUNS

MAKES 15

Preparation: 30 minutes, plus sponging and rising
Cooking time: 15–18 minutes, plus cooling

100ml (3½fl oz) warm milk, plus extra to glaze
15g (½oz) fresh yeast or 7g sachet (2 tsp) traditional dried yeast
50g (2oz) golden caster sugar, plus extra to glaze
350g (12oz) strong plain white flour, sifted, plus extra to dust
pinch of salt
pinch of ground cinnamon
pinch of freshly grated nutmeg
25g (1oz) chopped mixed candied peel
125g (4oz) mixed raisins, sultanas and currants
25g (1oz) butter, melted and cooled until tepid
1 medium egg, beaten
vegetable oil to grease

PER BUN
140 cals; 2g fat (of which 1g saturates); 28g carbohydrate; 0.2g salt

1 Mix the warm milk with an equal quantity of warm water. Put the yeast into a small bowl with 1 tbsp of the warm liquid and 1 tsp sugar and set aside for 5 minutes.
2 Put 225g (8oz) flour and the salt into a large bowl, make a well in the centre and pour in the yeast mixture. Cover with a clean teatowel and leave in a warm place for 20 minutes to 'sponge'.
3 Mix the remaining flour and sugar together with the spices, peel and dried fruit. Add to the yeast mixture with the melted butter and egg. Mix thoroughly to form a soft dough, adding a little more liquid if needed. Put the dough into a lightly oiled bowl, cover and leave to rise in a warm place for 1–1½ hours until doubled in size.
4 Knock back the dough and knead lightly on a lightly floured surface for 1–2 minutes. Divide the dough into 15 equal-sized pieces and shape into buns. Put well apart on a large oiled baking sheet. Make a deep cross on the top of each one with a sharp knife, then cover with a teatowel and leave in a warm place for about 30 minutes until doubled in size.
5 Preheat the oven to 220°C (200°C fan oven) mark 7. Brush the buns with milk and sprinkle with sugar, then bake for 15–18 minutes until they sound hollow when tapped underneath. Transfer to a wire rack and leave to cool. Serve warm.

VARIATION
Rather than mark crosses on the buns, brush with beaten egg to glaze, then top each with a pastry cross and glaze again. Bake as above.

STRAWBERRY SAVARIN

CUTS INTO 6 SLICES

Preparation: 15 minutes, plus standing
Cooking time: 40–45 minutes, plus cooling

oil to grease
15g (½oz) fresh yeast or 1½ tsp dried yeast
3 tbsp tepid milk
2 medium eggs, lightly beaten
50g (2oz) butter, melted and cooled
200g (7oz) plain white flour
1 tbsp caster sugar
25g (1oz) desiccated coconut
6 tbsp redcurrant jelly or sieved strawberry jam
5 tbsp lemon juice
450g (1lb) strawberries, hulled and quartered
soured cream to serve

PER SLICE

275 cals; 12g fat (of which 7g saturates); 39g carbohydrate; 0.2g salt

1   Lightly oil a 1.3 litre (2¼ pint) savarin tin or ring mould and turn it upside down on kitchen paper to drain off the excess oil.
2   Blend the fresh yeast with the milk. If using dried yeast, sprinkle it on to the milk and leave in a warm place for 30 minutes or until frothy. Gradually beat the eggs and butter into the yeast liquid.
3   Mix the flour in a bowl with the sugar and coconut. With a wooden spoon, gradually stir in the yeast mixture to form a thick smooth batter. Beat together thoroughly.
4   Turn into the prepared tin, cover with oiled clingfilm and leave in a warm place for about 1 hour until the savarin is nearly doubled in size. Preheat the oven to 190°C (170°C fan oven) mark 5.
5   Bake the savarin for 35–40 minutes until golden. Turn out on to a wire rack placed over a large plate. Put the jelly or jam and lemon juice into a small pan over a low heat.
6   When the jelly or jam is melted, spoon it over the warm savarin until well glazed, allowing any excess to collect on the plate under the wire rack. Transfer the savarin to a serving plate.
7   Return the excess jelly mixture to the pan, add the strawberries and stir to coat. Remove from the heat and cool for 15–20 minutes until almost set, then spoon into the middle of the savarin. Serve warm or cold with soured cream.

VARIATIONS
Strawberry babas:
Divide the yeast batter among six 9cm (3½ inch) ring tins. Leave to rise until the moulds are nearly two-thirds full, then bake for 15–20 minutes. Replace the lemon juice with brandy, soak each baba well and place on individual plates. Finish with strawberries and soured cream as left.

Rum babas:
Make as strawberry babas but soak the warm babas in a rum syrup made with 8 tbsp clear honey, 8 tbsp water and rum or rum essence to taste. Serve filled with whipped cream.

STRAWBERRY SAVARIN

●●●●●●●●●●●●●●●●●●●●●●●●●●●●●●●●●●

CUTS INTO 6 SLICES

Preparation: 15 minutes, plus standing
Cooking time: 40–45 minutes, plus cooling

oil to grease
15g (½oz) fresh yeast or 1½ tsp dried yeast
3 tbsp tepid milk
2 medium eggs, lightly beaten
50g (2oz) butter, melted and cooled
200g (7oz) plain white flour
1 tbsp caster sugar
25g (1oz) desiccated coconut
6 tbsp redcurrant jelly or sieved strawberry jam
5 tbsp lemon juice
450g (1lb) strawberries, hulled and quartered
soured cream to serve

PER SLICE
275 cals; 12g fat (of which 7g saturates); 39g carbohydrate; 0.2g salt

1 Lightly oil a 1.3 litre (2¼ pint) savarin tin or ring mould and turn it upside down on kitchen paper to drain off the excess oil.
2 Blend the fresh yeast with the milk. If using dried yeast, sprinkle it on to the milk and leave in a warm place for 30 minutes or until frothy. Gradually beat the eggs and butter into the yeast liquid.
3 Mix the flour in a bowl with the sugar and coconut. With a wooden spoon, gradually stir in the yeast mixture to form a thick smooth batter. Beat together thoroughly.
4 Turn into the prepared tin, cover with oiled clingfilm and leave in a warm place for about 1 hour until the savarin is nearly doubled in size. Preheat the oven to 190°C (170°C fan oven) mark 5.
5 Bake the savarin for 35–40 minutes until golden. Turn out on to a wire rack placed over a large plate. Put the jelly or jam and lemon juice into a small pan over a low heat.
6 When the jelly or jam is melted, spoon it over the warm savarin until well glazed, allowing any excess to collect on the plate under the wire rack. Transfer the savarin to a serving plate.
7 Return the excess jelly mixture to the pan, add the strawberries and stir to coat. Remove from the heat and cool for 15–20 minutes until almost set, then spoon into the middle of the savarin. Serve warm or cold with soured cream.

VARIATIONS
Strawberry babas:
Divide the yeast batter among six 9cm (3½ inch) ring tins. Leave to rise until the moulds are nearly two-thirds full, then bake for 15–20 minutes. Replace the lemon juice with brandy, soak each baba well and place on individual plates. Finish with strawberries and soured cream as left.

Rum babas:
Make as strawberry babas but soak the warm babas in a rum syrup made with 8 tbsp clear honey, 8 tbsp water and rum or rum essence to taste. Serve filled with whipped cream.

PUDDINGS

ROASTED FRUIT

● ●

SERVES 4

Preparation: 10 minutes
Cooking time: about 30 minutes

4 ripe peaches
150ml (¼ pint) orange juice
100ml (3½fl oz) dessert wine, such as Muscat de Beaumes de Venise
    (optional)
4 figs, trimmed
2 tbsp clear honey
150g (5oz) blueberries
crème fraîche or vanilla ice cream to serve

PER SERVING
140 cals; 0.5g fat (of which 0g saturates); 30g carbohydrate; 0.2g salt

1 Preheat the oven to 200°C (180°C fan oven) mark 6. Halve the peaches and remove
   and discard the stones. Arrange cut-side up in a medium roasting tin or heatproof
   serving dish. Pour the orange juice and Muscat, if using, over them and roast for
   15 minutes.
2 Meanwhile, put the figs on a board and cut each into quarters, leaving them attached
   at the base. Nestle in among the peach halves and drizzle the honey over. Return to
   the oven for 10 minutes or until all the fruit is tender.
3 Preheat the grill to medium. Scatter the blueberries over the roasted fruit and grill for
   1–2 minutes until the berries have burst and released some of their juice. Serve
   immediately with crème fraîche or vanilla ice cream.

BAKED APRICOTS WITH CARAMELISED NUTS

• •

SERVES 4

Preparation: 20 minutes
Cooking time: 45–50 minutes, plus cooling

700g (1½lb) firm apricots
50g (2oz) butter
125g (4oz) caster sugar
100ml (3½fl oz) orange juice
vanilla ice cream to serve (optional)

CARAMELISED NUTS
75g (3oz) whole almonds, skinned
125g (4oz) caster sugar

PER SERVING
419 cals; 21g fat (of which 7g saturates); 55g carbohydrate; 0.2g salt

1 Preheat the oven to 200°C (180°C fan oven) mark 6. Slit the apricots down one side (so they still look whole) and remove the stones. Put the apricots into an ovenproof dish. Gently melt the butter and sugar in a pan, stirring occasionally, until golden; remove from the heat. Carefully stir in the orange juice (it may splutter as the sugar hardens into lumps). Return the mixture to a low heat and stir until the sugar has dissolved, then pour over the apricots.

2 Bake in the oven for 45 minutes or until the apricots are just soft, spooning the liquid over the fruit from time to time. Set aside and leave to cool. (Remove the skins at this stage, if you like.)

3 To make the caramelised nuts, put the almonds into a pan of cold water, bring to the boil and simmer for 2 minutes. Drain and cut the almonds into thick shreds (they will now be soft enough to chop without splintering). Put under a hot grill and toast until golden.

4 Put the sugar and 150ml (¼ pint) water into a pan, bring to the boil and bubble until the syrup turns a deep golden caramel. Take the pan off the heat and add 4 tbsp warm water. Return the pan to the heat and cook gently until the sugar has dissolved. Allow the mixture to cool, then stir in the almonds. Serve the apricots with scoops of vanilla ice cream, if you like, with the caramelised nuts spooned over the top.

NOTES
• If the caramelised almond mixture sets, put back on the heat to warm slightly before spooning over the apricots.
• For convenience, prepare ahead. Complete the recipe to the end of step 2, then caramelise the nuts as in step 3. Spoon the almonds over the apricots, then cool, cover and chill for up to three days. To use, warm the apricots and almonds in a shallow pan until the syrup melts. Complete the recipe.

FREEZING TIP
To freeze, complete the recipe to the end of step 1, then cool, wrap and freeze. To use, thaw the apricots for 4 hours or overnight at cool room temperature. Complete the recipe.

BAKED APPLES WITH OATS AND BLUEBERRIES

● ● ● ● ● ● ● ● ● ● ● ● ● ● ● ● ● ● ●

SERVES 4

Preparation: 15 minutes

Cooking time: 30–40 minutes

4 Bramley apples
25g (1oz) pecan nuts, chopped
25g (1oz) rolled oats
50g (2oz) blueberries
2 tbsp light muscovado sugar
4 tbsp orange juice

PER SERVING

164 cals; 5g fat (of which trace saturates); 29g carbohydrate; 0g salt

1 Preheat the oven to 200°C (180°C fan oven) mark 6. Core the apples, then use a sharp knife to score around the middle of each (this will stop the apple from collapsing). Put the apples into a roasting tin.
2 Put the pecan nuts into a bowl together with the oats, blueberries and sugar. Mix together, then spoon into the apples, pour 1 tbsp orange juice over each apple and bake in the oven for 30–40 minutes until the apples are soft.

CHERRY CLAFOUTIS

SERVES 6

Preparation: 20 minutes, plus soaking
Cooking time: about 1 hour

350g (12oz) cherries, pitted
3 tbsp Kirsch
125g (4oz) golden caster sugar
4 large eggs
25g (1oz) plain flour, sifted
150ml (¼ pint) milk
150ml (¼ pint) double cream
1 tsp vanilla extract
a little butter to grease

PER SERVING

326 cals; 18g fat (of which 10g saturates); 33g carbohydrate; 0.2g salt

1 Put the cherries into a bowl with the Kirsch and 1 tbsp sugar. Mix together, cover and set aside for 1 hour.

2 Meanwhile, whisk together the eggs, 100g (3½oz) sugar and the flour in a bowl. Put the milk and cream into a small pan and bring to the boil. Pour on to the egg mixture and whisk until combined. Stir in the vanilla extract, then strain into a bowl. Cover and set aside for 30 minutes. Preheat the oven to 180°C (160°C fan oven) mark 4.

3 Lightly grease a 1.7 litre (3 pint) shallow ovenproof dish and sprinkle with the remaining sugar. Spoon the Kirsch-soaked cherries into the dish. Whisk the batter again, then pour it over the cherries. Bake for 50 minutes–1 hour until golden and just set. Serve warm.

VARIATION

For an autumnal clafoutis, replace the cherries with blackberries, the Kirsch with blackberry or blackcurrant liqueur and the vanilla with ¼ tsp ground cinnamon.

PEAR AND BLACKBERRY CRUMBLE

● ● ● ● ● ● ● ● ● ● ● ● ● ● ● ● ● ● ● ●

SERVES 6

Preparation: 20 minutes
Cooking time: 35–45 minutes

450g (1lb) pears, peeled, cored and chopped, tossed with the
    juice of 1 lemon
225g (8oz) golden caster sugar
1 tsp mixed spice
450g (1lb) blackberries
100g (3½oz) butter, chopped, plus extra to grease
225g (8oz) plain flour
75g (3oz) ground almonds
cream, custard or ice cream to serve

PER SERVING

525 cals; 21g fat (of which 9g saturates); 81g carbohydrate; 0.3g salt

1 Put the pears and lemon juice into a bowl, add 100g (3½oz)
   sugar and the mixed spice, then add the blackberries and toss
   thoroughly to coat.
2 Preheat the oven to 200°C (180°C fan oven) mark 6. Lightly
   grease a 1.8 litre (3¼ pint) shallow dish, then carefully tip the
   fruit into the dish in an even layer.
3 Put the butter, flour, ground almonds and the remaining sugar
   into a food processor and pulse until the mixture begins to
   resemble breadcrumbs. Tip into a bowl and bring parts of it
   together with your hands to make lumps. Spoon the crumble
   topping evenly over the fruit, then bake for 35–45 minutes
   until the fruit is tender and the crumble is golden and bubbling.
   Serve with cream, custard or ice cream.

VARIATION
Use apples instead of pears.

APPLE CRUMBLE

SERVES 4

Preparation: 15 minutes
Cooking time: 45 minutes

125g (4oz) plain flour
50g (2oz) unsalted butter, cubed
50g (2oz) golden caster sugar
450g (1lb) apples, peeled, cored and sliced
custard or double cream to serve

PER SERVING

425 cals; 18g fat (of which 7g saturates); 74g carbohydrate; 0.3g salt

1 Preheat the oven to 180°C (160°C fan oven) mark 4. Put the flour into a bowl, add
   the butter and rub in with your fingertips until the mixture resembles fine
   breadcrumbs. Stir in half the sugar. Put to one side.
2 Arrange half the apples in a 1.1 litre (2 pint) pie dish and sprinkle with the rest of the
   sugar. Add the remaining apple slices to the dish. Spoon the crumble mixture over
   the fruit.
3 Bake in the oven for about 45 minutes until the fruit is soft. Serve hot with custard
   or a drizzle of double cream.

STEAMED SYRUP
SPONGE PUDDINGS

● ●

SERVES 4

Preparation: 20 minutes
Cooking time: 35 minutes or 1½ hours

125g (4oz) butter, softened, plus extra to grease
3 tbsp golden syrup
125g (4oz) golden caster sugar
few drops of vanilla extract
2 medium eggs, beaten
175g (6oz) self-raising flour, sifted
about 3 tbsp milk
custard or cream to serve

PER SERVING

580 cals; 29g fat (of which 17g saturates); 76g carbohydrate; 0.7g salt

1 Half-fill a steamer or large pan with water and put it on to boil.
   Grease four 300ml (½ pint) basins or a 900ml (1½ pint)
   pudding basin and spoon the golden syrup into the bottom.
2 In a bowl, cream the butter and sugar together until pale and
   fluffy. Stir in the vanilla extract. Add the eggs, a little at a time,
   beating well after each addition.
3 Using a metal spoon, fold in half the flour, then fold in the rest
   with enough milk to give a dropping consistency. Spoon the
   mixture into the prepared pudding basin(s).
4 Cover with greased and pleated greaseproof paper and foil
   and secure with string. Steam for 35 minutes for individual
   puddings or 1½ hours for one large pudding, checking the
   water level from time to time and topping up with boiling
   water as necessary. Turn out on to warmed plates and serve
   with custard or cream.

VARIATIONS
Steamed jam sponge puddings:
Put 4 tbsp raspberry or blackberry jam into the bottom of the
basins instead of the syrup.

Steamed chocolate sponge puddings:
Omit the golden syrup. Blend 4 tbsp cocoa powder with 2 tbsp
hot water, then gradually beat into the creamed mixture before
adding the eggs.

STICKY TOFFEE PUDDINGS

• • • • • • • • • • • • • • • • • •

SERVES 4

Preparation: 20 minutes
Cooking time: 25–30 minutes, plus resting

1 tbsp golden syrup
1 tbsp black treacle
150g (5oz) butter, softened
25g (1oz) pecan nuts or walnuts, finely ground
75g (3oz) self-raising flour
125g (4oz) caster sugar
2 large eggs, beaten
cream or custard to serve

PER SERVING
565 cals; 38g fat (of which 21g saturates); 53g carbohydrate; 0.9g salt

1 Preheat the oven to 180°C (160°C fan oven) mark 4. Put the syrup, treacle and 25g (1oz) butter into a bowl and beat until smooth. Divide the mixture among four 150ml (¼ pint) timbales or ramekins and set aside.
2 Put the nuts into a bowl, sift in the flour and mix together well.
3 Put the remaining butter and the sugar into a food processor and blend briefly. (Alternatively, use a hand-held electric whisk.) Add the eggs and the flour mixture and blend or mix again for 30 seconds. Spoon the mixture into the timbales or ramekins, covering the syrup mixture on the bottom. Bake for 25–30 minutes until risen and golden.
4 Remove the puddings from the oven and leave to rest for 5 minutes, then unmould on to warmed plates. Serve immediately with cream or custard.

STEAMED LEMON PUDDINGS

SERVES 6

Preparation: 20 minutes
Cooking time: 40 minutes, plus standing

175g (6oz) unsalted butter, softened, plus extra to grease
6 tbsp lemon curd
175g (6oz) golden caster sugar
3 medium eggs
finely grated zest and juice of ½ large lemon
175g (6oz) self-raising flour
2 tsp baking powder
icing sugar to dust
Vanilla Custard to serve (see page 316)

PER SERVING (WITHOUT CUSTARD)

532 cals; 29g fat (of which 16g saturates); 66g carbohydrate; 0.6g salt

1 Preheat the oven to 180°C (160°C fan oven) mark 4. Grease six 200ml (7fl oz) dariole moulds and put 1 tbsp lemon curd in each.
2 Put the butter and caster sugar into a bowl and, using a hand-held electric whisk, beat until fluffy. Beat in the eggs, lemon zest and juice. Using a metal spoon, fold in the flour and baking powder.
3 Spoon the mixture into the prepared moulds, level the tops and cover each with a disc of greaseproof paper, then wrap in foil. Put the puddings into a roasting tin and pour in enough hot water to come halfway up the sides of the moulds. Cook for 40 minutes or until risen and cooked in the centre.
4 Lift the puddings out of the tin and leave to stand for 10 minutes. Run a palette knife around the edge of each dariole mould and turn out on to individual plates.
5 Dust with icing sugar and serve with vanilla custard.

FREEZING TIP
To freeze, complete the recipe to the end of step 4 up to three months ahead, then turn out the puddings into a freezerproof container, cool and freeze. To use, thaw the puddings at cool room temperature for 45 minutes. Preheat the oven to 200°C (180°C fan oven) mark 6. Grease an ovenproof dish. Put the puddings in the dish, lemon curd-side up, drizzle 5 tbsp water over all and cover loosely with foil. Reheat for 30–35 minutes, turn out on to plates and serve as in step 5.

SPOTTED DICK

● ●

SERVES 4

Preparation: 15 minutes
Cooking time: 2 hours

125g (4oz) fresh breadcrumbs
75g (3oz) self-raising flour, plus extra to dust
75g (3oz) shredded suet
50g (2oz) caster sugar
175g (6oz) currants
finely grated zest of 1 lemon
5 tbsp milk
butter to grease
custard to serve

PER SERVING

502 calories; 18g fat (of which 10g saturates); 84g carbohydrate; 0.8g salt

1 Half-fill a preserving pan or large saucepan with water and put on to boil.
2 Place the breadcrumbs, flour, suet, sugar, currants and lemon zest in a bowl and stir well until thoroughly mixed. Pour in the milk and stir until well blended. Using one hand, bring the ingredients together to form a soft, slightly sticky dough.
3 Turn the dough out on to a lightly floured surface and knead gently until just smooth. Shape into a neat roll about 15cm (6 inch) in length.
4 Make a 5cm (2 inch) pleat across a clean teatowel or pudding cloth (or pleat together sheets of greased greaseproof paper and strong foil). Encase the roll in the cloth or foil, pleating the open edges tightly together. Tie the ends securely with string to form a cracker shape. Make a string handle across the top. Lower the suet roll into the pan of boiling water and boil for 2 hours, topping up with boiling water as necessary.
5 Using the string handle, lift the spotted dick out of the water. Place on a wire rack standing over a plate and allow excess moisture to drain off.
6 Snip the string and gently roll the pudding out of the cloth or foil on to a warmed serving plate. Serve sliced, with custard.

FIG, ORANGE AND CRANBERRY CHRISTMAS PUDDING

SERVES 8

Preparation: 20 minutes, plus overnight soaking
Cooking time: 4½–5 hours

125g (4oz) each sultanas, currants and raisins
75g (3oz) dried cranberries
75g (3oz) dried figs, finely chopped
75ml (3fl oz) orange liqueur, such as Cointreau
zest and juice of 1 orange
butter to grease
1 pear
2 medium eggs
50g (2oz) each shredded vegetarian suet and self-raising flour
75g (3oz) fresh white breadcrumbs
½ tsp each mixed spice and ground cinnamon
pinch of freshly grated nutmeg
100g (3½oz) soft dark brown sugar
25g (1oz) brazil nuts, roughly chopped (optional)

PER SERVING

435 cals; 12g fat (of which 5g saturates); 75g carbohydrate; 0.8g salt

1 Put the dried fruit into a large non-metallic bowl and stir in the liqueur, orange zest and juice. Cover and leave to soak overnight at room temperature.

2 Lightly grease a 1 litre (1¾ pint) pudding basin and line the bottom with a circle of baking parchment. Lay a 35.5cm (14 inch) square of foil on top of a square of baking parchment the same size. Fold a 4cm (1½ inch) pleat down the centre of both and set aside.

3 Core the pear, then grate into the soaked fruit mixture. Beat the eggs and add to the bowl, then add all the remaining ingredients and stir well. Spoon into the prepared basin, pressing down firmly, and level the top. Put the pleated foil square (foil-side up) on top of the pudding and smooth down to cover. Using a long length of string, securely tie down the square just under the lip of the basin and knot it. Bring the excess string over the top of the bowl and tie it to the string under the lip on the other side to make a handle. Scrunch the edge of the parchment up underneath the foil.

4 Put an upturned heatproof saucer into a deep pan and balance the pudding on top. Pour in enough water to come halfway up the sides of the basin, cover the pan with a tight-fitting lid and bring to a simmer. Cook for 4½–5 hours, checking the water level regularly and topping up as necessary with boiling water. Remove the pudding from the pan and cool. Once it is cold, wrap the entire basin tightly in clingfilm and a layer of foil. Store in a cool, dark place for up to two months.

TO REHEAT

Remove the foil and clingfilm wrapping. Re-cover the top of the basin with baking parchment and foil. Cook the pudding as in step 4 for 2 hours. Discard the foil and parchment. Slide a knife around the edge of the pudding, then turn out on to a plate and leave to stand for 15 minutes before serving.

BREAD AND BUTTER PUDDING

● ● ● ● ● ● ● ● ● ● ● ● ● ● ● ● ● ●

SERVES 4

Preparation: 10 minutes, plus soaking
Cooking time: 30–40 minutes

50g (2oz) butter, softened, plus extra to grease
275g (10oz) white farmhouse bread, cut into 1cm (½ inch) slices,
  crusts removed
50g (2oz) raisins or sultanas
3 medium eggs
450ml (¾ pint) milk
3 tbsp golden icing sugar, plus extra to dust

PER SERVING
450 cals; 13g fat (of which 5g saturates); 70g carbohydrate; 1.1g salt

1 Lightly grease four 300ml (½ pint) gratin dishes or one 1.1 litre
  (2 pint) ovenproof dish. Butter the bread, then cut into
  quarters to make triangles. Arrange the bread in the dish(es)
  and sprinkle with the raisins or sultanas.
2 Beat the eggs, milk and sugar in a bowl. Pour the mixture over
  the bread and leave to soak for 10 minutes. Preheat the oven
  to 180°C (160°C fan oven) mark 4.
3 Put the pudding(s) in the oven and bake for 30–40 minutes.
  Dust with icing sugar to serve.

QUICK CHOCOLATE PUDDINGS

● ● ● ● ● ● ● ● ● ● ● ● ● ● ● ● ● ● ●

SERVES 4

Preparation: 15 minutes
Cooking time: 12–15 minutes

100g (3½oz) butter, plus extra to grease
100g (3½oz) golden caster sugar, plus extra to dust
100g (3½oz) plain chocolate (at least 70% cocoa solids), broken
   into pieces
2 large eggs
20g (¾oz) plain flour
icing sugar to dust

PER SERVING

468 cals; 31g fat (of which 19g saturates); 46g carbohydrate; 0.6g salt

1 Preheat the oven to 200°C (180°C fan oven) mark 6. Grease
   four 200ml (7fl oz) ramekins and dust with sugar. Melt the
   chocolate and butter in a heatproof bowl set over a pan of
   gently simmering water, making sure the base of the bowl
   doesn't touch the water. Take the bowl off the pan and leave to
   cool for 5 minutes.
2 Whisk the eggs, caster sugar and flour together in a bowl
   until smooth. Fold in the chocolate mixture and pour into the
   ramekins.
3 Stand the dishes on a baking tray and bake for 12–15 minutes
   until the puddings are puffed and set on the outside, but still
   runny inside. Turn out, dust with icing sugar and serve
   immediately.

BAKED ALASKA

LONG FREEZING REQUIRED

SERVES 8

Preparation: 30 minutes, plus freezing
Cooking time: 3–4 minutes

1 large sponge flan case, 25.5cm (10 inch) diameter
5 tbsp orange juice
7 tbsp jam – any kind
1.5 litre tub vanilla ice cream
6 large egg whites
pinch of cream of tartar
pinch of salt
275g (10oz) golden caster sugar

PER SERVING
659 cals; 30g fat (of which 17g saturates); 91g carbohydrate; 0.5g salt

1 Put the flan case on an ovenproof plate. Spoon the orange
   juice over the sponge, then spread with the jam. Scoop the
   ice cream on top of the jam, then put in the freezer for at least
   30 minutes.
2 Put the egg whites into a large, clean, grease-free bowl and
   whisk until stiff. Beat in the cream of tartar and salt. Using a
   large spoon, fold in the sugar, 1 tbsp at a time, then whisk until
   very thick and shiny.
3 Spoon the meringue over the ice cream to cover, making sure
   that the meringue is sealed to the flan case edge all the way
   round. Freeze for at least 1 hour or overnight.
4 Preheat the oven to 230°C (210°C fan oven) mark 8. Bake
   for 3–4 minutes until the meringue is tinged golden brown.
   Serve immediately. If the Baked Alaska has been in the freezer
   overnight, bake and leave to stand for about 15 minutes before
   serving.

RICE PUDDING

● ● ● ● ● ● ● ● ● ● ● ● ● ● ● ● ●

SERVES 6

Preparation: 5 minutes
Cooking time: 1½ hours

butter to grease
125g (4oz) short-grain pudding rice
1.1 litres (2 pints) milk
50g (2oz) golden caster sugar
1 tsp vanilla extract
grated zest of 1 orange (optional)
freshly grated nutmeg to taste

PER SERVING

239 cals; 8g fat (of which 5g saturates); 34g carbohydrate; 0.2g salt

1 Preheat the oven to 170°C (150°C fan oven) mark 3. Lightly grease a 1.7 litre (3 pint) ovenproof dish.
2 Put the rice, milk, sugar, vanilla extract and orange zest, if using, into the dish and stir everything together. Grate the nutmeg over the top of the mixture.
3 Bake the pudding in the middle of the oven for 1½ hours or until the top is golden brown.

STRAWBERRY PAVLOVA WITH ROSEWATER SYRUP

●●

SERVES 10

Preparation: 20 minutes
Cooking time: about 50 minutes, plus cooling

10 medium egg whites
600g (1lb 5oz) caster sugar
1¾ tbsp cornflour
1kg (2¼lb) strawberries, hulled
150ml (5fl oz) dessert wine, such as Muscat de Beaumes de Venise
1 tsp rosewater
600ml (1 pint) double cream
3 tbsp icing sugar, sifted

PER SERVING

614 cals; 32g fat (of which 20g saturates); 78g carbohydrate; 0.3g salt

1 Preheat the oven to 150°C (130°C fan oven) mark 2. Line a large baking sheet with baking parchment. Use a pencil to draw a 28cm (11 inch) diameter circle on the parchment, then flip it over so the pencil mark is underneath.

2 Using electric beaters, whisk the egg whites in a large, grease-free bowl until stiff but not dry. Gradually add 550g (1¼lb) caster sugar, whisking all the time, until the mixture is stiff and glossy. Quickly beat in 1 tbsp cornflour.

3 Spoon the mixture on to the prepared baking tray within the marked circle, pushing it into peaks at the edges of the circle. Bake for 40 minutes or until the meringue is firm to the touch and peels away from the parchment. Transfer to a rack and leave to cool.

4 Meanwhile, put 200g (7oz) strawberries with the wine, remaining caster sugar and the rosewater into a pan. Heat and simmer gently for 5 minutes. Blend until smooth, then push through a fine sieve, discarding the pips. Return the mixture to the pan and whisk in the remaining cornflour. Heat gently for 3–4 minutes until the syrup thickens, whisking constantly to remove any lumps. Take off the heat and leave to cool.

5 Transfer the cooled meringue to a serving plate. Gently whip the cream with the icing sugar until it just holds its shape. Dollop on top of the meringue, then pile on the remaining strawberries. Drizzle the cooled syrup over and serve.

NOTE

For convenience, prepare ahead. Cook the meringue, make the strawberry syrup and hull the strawberries up to one day ahead. Cool the meringue on the baking sheet, then cover with clingfilm and store at room temperature. Cool the syrup, then cover and chill. Keep the hulled strawberries covered in the fridge. Whip the cream mixture up to 2 hours ahead, then chill. To serve, bring the syrup, strawberries and cream up to room temperature, then complete the recipe.

CELEBRATION CAKES

BEST EVER CHRISTMAS CAKE

CUTS INTO 24 SLICES

Preparation: 30 minutes, plus soaking
Cooking time: about 4 hours, plus cooling

500g (1lb 2oz) sultanas
400g (14oz) raisins
150g (5oz) each Agen prunes and dried figs, roughly chopped
200g (7oz) dried apricots, roughly chopped
zest and juice of 2 oranges
200ml (7fl oz) hazelnut liqueur, such as Frangelico Hazelnut Liqueur, plus extra to drizzle
250g (9oz) unsalted butter, softened, plus extra to grease
150g (5oz) each dark muscovado and light brown soft sugar
200g (7oz) plain flour, sifted
1 tsp ground cinnamon
1 tsp mixed spice
¼ tsp ground cloves
¼ tsp freshly grated nutmeg
pinch of salt
4 large eggs, beaten
100g (3½oz) toasted, blanched hazelnuts, roughly chopped
40g (1½oz) toasted pinenuts
1 tbsp brandy (optional)

PER SLICE
375 cals; 14g fat (of which 6g saturates); 56g carbohydrate; 0.4g salt

1 Put the fruit into a non-metallic bowl and stir in the orange zest and juice and the hazelnut liqueur. Cover and leave to soak overnight or, preferably, up to 3 days.

2 Preheat the oven to 140°C (120°C fan oven) mark 1. Grease a 23cm (9 inch) cake tin and double-line with greaseproof paper, making sure the paper comes at least 5cm (2 inch) above the top of the tin. Then wrap a double layer of greaseproof paper around the outside of the tin, securing with string – this will stop the cake burning.

3 Using a hand-held electric mixer, beat together the butter and sugars in a large bowl until light and fluffy – this should take about 5 minutes.

4 In a separate bowl, sift together the flour, spices and salt. Beat 2 tbsp of the flour mixture into the butter and sugar, then gradually add the eggs, making sure the mixture doesn't curdle. If it looks as if it might be about to, add a little more flour.

5 Using a large metal spoon, fold the remaining flour into the mixture, followed by the soaked fruit and the nuts. Tip into the prepared tin and level the surface. Using the end of the spoon, make a hole in the centre of the mix, going right down to the base of the tin – this will stop the top of the cake rising into a dome shape as it cooks. Bake for 4 hours or until a skewer inserted into the centre comes out clean. Cover with foil if it is browning too quickly. Leave to cool in the tin for 10 minutes, then turn out on to a wire rack, keeping the greaseproof paper wrapped around the outside of the cake, and leave to cool completely.

6 To store, leave the cold cake in its greaseproof paper. Wrap a few layers of clingfilm around it, then cover with foil. Store in a cool place in an airtight container. After two weeks, unwrap the cake, prick all over and pour over 1 tbsp of hazelnut liqueur, or brandy if you prefer. Rewrap and store as before. Ice up to three days before serving (see opposite).

NOTE
For convenience, prepare ahead. Complete the recipe up to three months ahead and store as in step 6. It can be doused in alcohol every week if you like a stronger taste.

ICING THE CAKE

• •

**MAKES ENOUGH TO COVER
A 23CM (9 INCH) CAKE**

Preparation: 30 minutes, plus drying
Cooking time: 3–4 minutes, plus cooling

4 tbsp apricot jam
1 fruit cake (see opposite)
sifted icing sugar to dust
450g packet ready-to-roll marzipan
vegetable oil to grease
150g (5oz) glacier mint sweets
500g packet royal icing sugar

75 x 2cm (30 x ¾ inch) silver ribbon
silver candles

PER SERVING (INCLUDING CAKE)

569 cals; 17g fat (of which 6g saturates); 100g carbohydrate; 0.2g salt

1   Gently heat the jam in a pan with 1 tbsp water until softened, then press through a sieve into a bowl to make a smooth glaze. Put the cake on a board and brush over the top and sides with the glaze.

2   Dust a rolling pin and worksurface with a little icing sugar and roll out the marzipan to a round about 15cm (6 inch) larger than the cake. Position over the cake and ease to fit around the sides, pressing out any creases. Trim off the excess around the base. Leave to dry for 24 hours.

3   Preheat the oven to 180°C (160°C fan oven) mark 4. Line a baking sheet with foil and brush lightly with oil. Unwrap the mints and put pairs of sweets on the baking sheet about 1cm (½ inch) apart, leaving 5cm (2 inch) of space between each pair, to allow room for them to spread as they melt. Cook for 3–4 minutes until the sweets have melted and are just starting to bubble around the edges. Leave to cool on the foil for 3–4 minutes until firm enough to be lifted off. Use kitchen scissors to snip the pieces into large slivers and shards.

4   Wrap the ribbon around the edge of the cake. Put the icing sugar in a bowl and make up according to packet instructions. Using a small palette knife, spread the icing over the top of the cake, flicking it into small peaks as you go. Then tease the edges of the icing down the sides of the cake to form icicles.

5   While the icing is still soft, push the mint shards into the top of the cake and insert the silver candles. Leave the cake to dry. Light the candles and serve.

TO STORE

Once cut into, store the cake in a container in a cool, dry place. It will keep for up to two weeks.

SIMNEL CAKE

● ●

CUTS INTO 12–16 SLICES

Preparation: 1½ hours
Cooking time: 2¾ hours, plus cooling and setting

250g (9oz) unsalted butter, softened, plus
    extra to grease
grated zest of 2 unwaxed lemons
250g (9oz) golden caster sugar
4 large eggs, beaten
250g (9oz) plain flour
½ tsp ground mixed spice
75g (3oz) ground almonds
50g (2oz) mixed candied peel, finely
    chopped
150g (5oz) currants
300g (11oz) sultanas

75g (3oz) natural glacé cherries, halved
100g (3½oz) icing sugar, plus extra to dust
600g (1lb 5oz) almond paste (see page
    313) or ready-made white marzipan
2 tbsp thin honey, warmed
1 medium egg, beaten, to glaze

PER SLICE

750–565 cals; 36–27g fat (of which 12–9g saturates);
104–78g carbohydrate; 0.5–0.4g salt

1 Preheat the oven to 170°C (150°C fan oven) mark 3. Grease a 20.5cm (8 inch) round, 7.5cm (3 inch) deep cake tin and line with greaseproof paper.
2 Using a freestanding mixer or hand-held electric whisk, beat the butter and lemon zest together until very soft. Gradually add the sugar and continue beating until light and fluffy. Slowly beat in the eggs until evenly incorporated.
3 Sift in the flour with the mixed spice, then add the ground almonds, candied peel, currants, sultanas and glacé cherries. Using a large metal spoon, fold the ingredients together, until evenly combined. Set aside.
4 Spoon just over half of the cake mixture into the prepared tin and level the surface. Roll out 200g (7oz) almond paste on a surface lightly dusted with icing sugar to an 18cm (7 inch) round.
5 Put the almond paste round on top of the mixture in the tin, then cover with the remaining cake mixture. Smooth the surface and make a slight hollow in the centre, then brush lightly with cold water. Wrap a double layer of brown paper around the outside of the tin (see step 2, page 288) and secure with string. Bake for 1¼ hours. Cover with greaseproof paper, lower the oven setting to 150°C (130°C fan oven) mark 2 and bake for a further 1½ hours or until cooked to the centre.
6 Cool in the tin for 1 hour, then turn out on to a wire rack and leave to cool completely. Wrap in greaseproof paper and foil and store in an airtight container for up to two weeks.
7 When ready to decorate, roll out 200g (7oz) almond paste to a 20.5cm (8 inch) round. Cut a 7.5cm (3 inch) round from the centre and add this piece to the remaining almond paste. Brush the top of the cake with honey, cover with the almond paste ring and press down. Crimp the edge with your fingers.
8 Divide the rest of the almond paste into 11 or 12 pieces (see note) and shape into oval balls. Brush the ring with the beaten egg, position the balls on top and brush them with egg. Put a disc of foil over the exposed centre of the cake, then put under a hot grill for 1–2 minutes to brown the almond paste.
9 Mix the icing sugar with 2–3 tbsp warm water to make a smooth icing. Remove the foil disc, then pour the icing on to the exposed centre and smooth it with a palette knife. Leave the icing to set. To finish, secure a yellow ribbon around the side of the cake.

NOTE
Simnel cake is the classic Easter celebration cake, its marzipan balls representing the disciples – either 11 or 12 – depending on whether you think Judas should be included.

GINGERBREAD HOUSE

OVERNIGHT PREPARATION NEEDED

MAKES 4 HOUSES

Preparation: 4 hours, plus 30 minutes chilling and 5 hours drying

Cooking time: 10 minutes

150g (5oz) butter, plus extra to grease
350g (12oz) plain white flour, sifted
1 tsp bicarbonate of soda
2 tbsp ground ginger
200g (7oz) light muscovado sugar
2 tbsp golden syrup
1 medium egg, beaten

DECORATION

200g (7oz) icing sugar, sifted
1 medium egg white
75g (3oz) assorted sweets

MATERIALS

Card to make the three templates:
roof: 10 x 6.5cm (4 x 2½in)
end wall: 10 x 6cm (4 x 2¼in)
side wall: 6 x 8cm (2¼ x 3¼in)
four 15cm (6in) cake boards covered in paper ribbon and cellophane

PER HOUSE

1000 cals; 34g fat (of which 20g saturates); 172g carbohydrate; 0.7g salt

1 Grease two baking sheets. Cut the card into templates for the roof and walls. Put the flour, bicarbonate of soda and ginger into a bowl. Rub in the butter until the mixture resembles breadcrumbs. Stir in the sugar. Warm the golden syrup in a pan, pour on to the flour with the beaten egg and stir. Bring together into a soft dough and knead until smooth. Divide into four pieces, wrap in clingfilm and chill for 15 minutes.

2 Roll out one piece of dough to 3mm (⅛ in) thick. Cut out two of each template. Put on to the baking sheets. Repeat with the remaining dough. Stamp out four hearts from the trimmings and skewer a hole in the top of each. Put on to the baking sheets. Chill for 15 minutes. Preheat the oven to 190°C (170°C fan oven) mark 5. Bake for 8–10 minutes until golden. While still warm, push a skewer through the holes. Leave on the baking sheets for 5 minutes, then transfer to a wire rack to cool completely.

3 To decorate, beat the icing sugar into the egg white until the mixture stands in peaks. Spoon into a piping bag and pipe windows and doors on the walls and squiggly lines on the roof. Leave to dry for 2 hours. Pipe icing along the edge of the side walls and stick to the end walls. Leave to dry for 1 hour, then place on a board and fill with sweets. Pipe icing along the top of each house and the roof pieces and press gently in position; hold for 1–2 minutes until secure.

NOTE

Pipe names on the heart-shaped gift tags and leave the house and tags to set for at least 2 hours. Wrap each gingerbread house in cellophane and tie with ribbon. Attach the gift tags with ribbon.

CLOWN CAKE

● ●

SERVES 15

Preparation: 45 minutes

25g (1oz) each of white, green, black and blue ready-to-roll icing
   (sugar paste)
50g (2oz) red ready-to-roll icing (sugar paste)
black and yellow writing icing
1 x white ready-iced 20.5cm (8 inch) sponge cake (see page 18)

PER SERVING

300 cals; 8g fat (of which 2g saturates); 55g carbohydrate; 0.1g salt

1 First make the shapes for the clown's face. Roll out the white
   ready-to-roll icing and cut out two ovals for eyes. Roll out half
   the red icing and cut out a crescent shape for the mouth. Mark
   a smiley line along the centre of the mouth with black writing
   icing. Knead the trimmings and the other piece of red icing
   together and roll into a ball for his nose. Roll out a small piece
   of green icing and, using a star-shaped cutter, stamp out two
   stars for his cheeks.

2 Brush the backs of the shapes with water and position on the
   cake. Roll out the black icing and cut out two small circles to
   make pupils for the eyes, then stick on to the white ovals. Use
   the black and yellow writing icing to give him eyebrows and a
   swirl of hair.

3 Roll out the blue icing and cut out two sides of a bow tie. Roll
   the trimmings into a ball and flatten slightly to make the centre
   knot. Fix the two bow-tie pieces to the bottom edge of the
   cake with writing icing. Position the knot on top. Use the
   yellow writing icing to pipe polka dots on the tie.

NOTE

For convenience, complete the recipe up to one day in advance.

CREEPY-CRAWLY CAKE

OVERNIGHT
PREPARATION
NEEDED

SERVES 12

Preparation: 1½ hours
Cooking time: 25–30 minutes, plus cooling and drying

butter to grease
1 x 4-egg quantity of chocolate Victoria sponge mixture
   (see page 11)
½ x quantity of chocolate buttercream icing (see page 314)

DECORATION
225g (8oz) white ready-to-roll icing (sugar paste)
assorted food colourings, including brown and black
red and black liquorice bootlaces and jelly creepy-crawly sweets,
   such as snakes and frogs
a little glacé icing (see page 312)
a chocolate matchstick (optional)

ICING
450g (1lb) icing sugar, sifted
225g (8oz) butter, softened
few drops of vanilla extract
green food colouring

PER SERVING
534 cals; 26 fat (of which 17g saturates); 76g carbohydrate; 0.6g salt

1 To make a trap door, use 125g (4oz) ready-to-roll icing. Knead in a few drops of brown food colouring and roll out to a thickness of 5mm (¼ inch), then use a small tumbler to cut out a circle. Place on a baking tray lined with baking parchment and leave in a cool place overnight to dry.

2 Use the remaining white and brown icing to make a selection of spiders and beetles, colouring the icing accordingly. Use the liquorice to make spiders' legs. Pipe eyes on the creatures with white glacé icing. Allow to dry overnight.

3 The next day, grease two 20.5cm (8 inch) round sandwich tins and line with greaseproof paper. Make and bake the sponge mixture according to the instructions on page 11. Cool in the tins for 5 minutes, then turn out on to a wire rack, remove the lining paper and leave to cool completely.

4 Sandwich the cold cakes together with chocolate buttercream. Cut out a hole 1cm (½ inch) deep and 6.5cm (2½ inch) wide in the centre of the cake. Discard (or eat) the trimmings.

5 For the icing, beat the icing sugar into the butter with the vanilla. Beat in the food colouring. Put the cake on a board or plate and cover with the icing. Secure the trap door over the hole in the middle of the cake. Prop open with a cocktail stick painted with brown food colouring, or a chocolate matchstick, if you like. Arrange the creatures over the cake, with some creepy-crawlies crawling out of the trap door. Leave to dry.

NOTE
For convenience, complete the recipe up to one day in advance.

GINGERBREAD FOOTBALLERS

● ● ● ● ● ● ● ● ● ● ● ● ● ● ● ● ● ● ● ●

MAKES 20

Preparation: 5 minutes, plus chilling

Cooking time: 12–15 minutes, plus cooling and setting

125g (4oz) cold butter, diced, plus extra to grease
350g (12oz) plain flour, plus extra to dust
1 tsp bicarbonate of soda
2 tsp ground ginger
175g (6oz) light soft brown sugar
4 tbsp golden syrup
1 medium egg, beaten
assorted writing icings
star and football decorations (optional)

PER BISCUIT

157 cals; 6g fat (of which 4g saturates); 26g carbohydrate; 0.2g salt

1 Lightly grease three baking sheets with butter. Sift the flour, bicarbonate of soda and ginger into a mixing bowl. Rub in the butter until the mixture resembles fine breadcrumbs, then stir in the sugar. (Alternatively, use a food processor.) Beat the syrup with the egg, then stir into the flour mixture and mix to make a dough. Knead until smooth, then divide in half and wrap in clingfilm. Chill for 30 minutes.

2 Preheat the oven to 190°C (170°C fan oven) mark 5. Turn out the dough on to a lightly floured surface and cut in half. Roll out each half until about 5mm (¼ inch) thick. Using a gingerbread man cutter, cut out shapes. Repeat with the second half of the dough. Re-roll the trimmings until all of the dough has been used. Put the gingerbread men on the prepared baking sheets.

3 Bake for 12–15 minutes until golden brown. Leave on the baking sheets to cool slightly, then transfer to wire racks and leave to cool completely.

4 When the gingerbread has cooled completely, decorate the footballers. Using black writing icing, give each man a pair of eyes and a dot for a nose. Use red icing for a mouth and black or yellow icing for hair. Choosing the colour(s) of your child's favourite football strip, draw an outline around the edge of the gingerbread to represent a shirt and shorts, then fill in the shirt with stripes if you like. Use contrasting icing to write a number on the front of each shirt. Decorate the shorts with stars, if you like, and attach footballs with a dot of writing icing. Leave to set for about 30 minutes. Remember to remove non-edible decorations before eating.

TO STORE
Store in an airtight container. They will keep for up to one week.

BAKING KNOW-HOW

BAKING EQUIPMENT

Not much in the way of specialist equipment is needed for baking, although one or two items in particular, such as a food processor and electric whisk, will make life much easier. Remember that kitchen equipment is subject to a great deal of wear and tear, so look for good-quality items. Below are the essentials when baking.

Scales Accurate measurement is essential when following most baking recipes. The electronic scale is the most accurate and can weigh up to 2kg (4½lb) or 5kg (11lb) in increments of 1–5g. Buy one with a flat platform on which you can put your bowl or measuring jug. Always set the scale to zero before adding the ingredients.

Measuring jugs, cups and spoons Jugs can be plastic or glass, and are available, marked with both metric and imperial, in sizes ranging from 500ml (18fl oz) to 2 litres (3½ pints), or even 3 litres (5¼ pints). Measuring cups are bought in sets of ¼, ⅓, ½ and 1 cups. A standard 1 cup measure is equivalent to about 250ml (9fl oz). Measuring spoons are useful for the smallest units and accurate spoon measurements go up to 15ml (1 tbsp). These may be in plastic or metal and often come in sets attached together on a ring.

Mixing bowls Stainless steel bowls work best when you are using a hand whisk, or when you need to place the bowl into a larger bowl filled with iced water for chilling down or to place it over simmering water (when melting chocolate, for example).

Plastic or glass bowls are best if you need to use them in the microwave. Bowls with gently tapered sides – much wider at the rim than at the base – will be useful for mixing dough.

Mixing spoons For general mixing, the cheap and sturdy wooden spoon still can't be beaten. The spoon should be stiff, so that it can cope with thick mixtures such as dough. In addition, a large metal spoon for folding ingredients together is also an invaluable item to have.

Other useful items These include spatulas, fine sieve, wire whisks, pastry brush, rolling pin, graters (fine and coarse), tape measure and paint brushes (for cake decorating).

BAKEWARE

As well as being thin enough to conduct heat quickly and efficiently, bakeware should be sturdy enough not to warp. Most bakeware is made from aluminium, and it may have enamel or non-stick coatings. A newer material for some bakeware is flexible, oven-safe silicone. It is safe to touch straight from the oven, is inherently non-stick and is also flexible – making it a lot easier to remove muffins and other bakes from their pans than it used to be.

Baking trays/Baking sheets Shallower than a roasting tin, these have many uses in baking. Choose ones that are large (but which fit comfortably in your oven) to avoid having to bake in batches. Buy the best you can afford.

Baking dishes Usually ceramic or Pyrex, you should have them in several sizes, ranging from 15–23cm (6–9 inch) to 25.5–35.5cm (10–14 inch).

Cake tins Available in many shapes and sizes, tins may be single-piece, loose-based or springform.

Loaf tins Available in various sizes, but one of the most useful is a 900g (2lb) tin.

Pie tins You should have both single-piece tins and loose-based tins for flans and pies.

Muffin tins These come in various sizes and depths and are available in both aluminium and silicone. If you make a lot of muffins and cupcakes it's worth investing in different types.

ELECTRICAL EQUIPMENT

Food processor Perfect for making breadcrumbs or pastry or for chopping large quantities of nuts. Most come with a number of attachments – dough hooks, graters, slicers.

Blenders Less versatile than food processors, but perfect for certain tasks, such as puréeing fruit. The traditional jug blender is great but some cooks prefer a 'stick' blender, which can be used directly in a pan, bowl or jug.

Freestanding mixers These powerful machines are particularly useful for bread-making and lengthy whisking, but they take up quite a lot of space on the worksurface.

Hand-held electric mixers and whisks Useful for creaming together butter and sugar in baking and for making meringues. They don't take up a lot of space and can be packed away easily.

Bread machines Kneading bread by hand doesn't take much time and effort, but bread machines are useful for making and baking bread if you have limited time and want to get on with something else. Doughs can also be prepared by the machine and then shaped and baked in the oven.

Ice-cream makers Even if you make ice cream only a few times a year, investing in a good machine will save lots of time and produce better results than an inferior model. The type with two freezing tubs enables you to make two flavours at once, or a larger quantity of a single flavour. A multi-speed ice-cream maker will make ice cream quickly and allow you to make other frozen desserts such as frozen yogurts and smoothies.

CAKE- AND BISCUIT-MAKING TECHNIQUES

Successful cake-making

The key to successful baking lies in using good-quality ingredients at the right temperature, measuring them accurately (using scales and measuring spoons) and following recipes very carefully. Weigh out all the ingredients before you start, using either metric or imperial measures, never a combination of the two. Check that all storecupboard ingredients to be used are well within their 'use-by' date. See also pages 308–311.

INGREDIENTS

FAT Unsalted butter gives the best results in most recipes. **Margarine** can be substituted in many recipes, although it doesn't lend such a good flavour, but **low-fat 'spreads'**, with their high water content, are not suitable. For most cake recipes, you need to use the fat at room temperature. If necessary you can soften it, cautiously, in the microwave.

EGGS Eggs should also be used at room temperature; if taken straight from the fridge they are more likely to curdle a cake mixture. Make sure you use the correct size – unless otherwise stated, medium eggs should be used in all the recipes. A fresh egg should feel heavy in your hand and will sink to the bottom of the bowl or float on its side when put into water. Older eggs, over two weeks old, will float vertically.

SUGAR Golden caster sugar is generally used for cakes, but for a richer colour and flavour, **light or dark muscovado sugars** can be substituted. **Icing sugar** is ideal for icings, frostings and buttercreams.

FLOUR Self-raising white flour is used in most cake recipes, as it provides a raising agent, whereas **plain white flour** is generally used for biscuits and cookies. **Plain or self-raising wholemeal** flour can be substituted, although the results will be darker and denser and nuttier in flavour. **Half white and half wholemeal** makes a good compromise if you want to incorporate extra fibre. If you sieve it before use, tip the bran left in the sieve into the bowl.

NUTS Some nuts can be bought ready-prepared, others need preparation. After nuts have been shelled, they are still coated with a skin, which, although edible, tastes bitter. This is easier to remove if the nuts are blanched or toasted. **To blanch**, put the shelled nuts in a bowl and cover with boiling water. Leave for 2 minutes, then drain. Remove the skins by rubbing the nuts in a teatowel or squeezing between your thumb and index finger.
Toasting also improves the flavour. Preheat the oven to 200°C (180°C fan oven) mark 6. Put the shelled nuts on a baking sheet in a single layer and bake for 8–15 minutes until the skins are lightly coloured. Remove the skins by rubbing the nuts in a teatowel. Unless you want very large pieces, the easiest way **to chop** nuts is to put the cold, skinned nuts in a food processor and pulse at 10-second intervals. Or, place a chopping board on a folded teatowel on the worksurface and use a cook's knife to chop to the size of coarse breadcrumbs. Only chop about 75g (3oz) of nuts at a time. Store in an airtight container for up to two weeks. **To slice** nuts, put them on a board and, using a cook's knife, carefully slice the nuts as thinly as required. **To make slivers**, carefully cut the slices to make narrow matchsticks.

  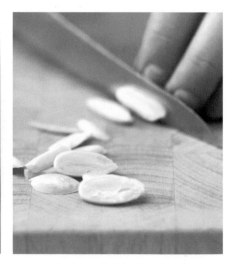

Nuts: blanching, toasting and cutting

Cake-making methods

METHODS

A variety of cakes can be prepared using three basic techniques: creaming (Victoria Sponge, page 10), all-in-one (Sticky Lemon Polenta Cake, page 25) and whisking (Whisked Sponge, page 12). These straightforward basic recipes can be adapted in several ways.

CAKE TINS

To ensure successsful home baking, check that you have the correct cake tin – the cake tin sizes quoted in the recipes refer to the base measurement – and line the tin properly where necessary. Allow at least 15 minutes to heat the oven to the correct oven temperature.

LINING TINS

Always line your cake tin with greaseproof paper – this will help to stop the cake sticking to the sides of the tin or burning (use baking parchment for roulades and meringues). Lightly grease the tin first to help keep the paper in place. Apply the butter with a small piece of greaseproof paper. Don't thickly grease the tin, as this will 'fry' the edges of the cake.

SQUARE TIN

1 Cut out a square of greaseproof paper slightly smaller than the base of the cake tin. Cut four strips each about 2cm (¾ inch) wider than the depth of the tin and fold up one of the longest edges of each strip by 1cm (½ inch).

2 Lightly grease the tin with butter, making sure it is coated on all sides and in the corners.

3 Cut one strip to the length of the side of the tin and press into place in one corner and then along the length of the strip, with the narrow folded section sitting on the base. Continue, cutting to fit into the corners, to cover all four sides.

4 Lay the square on the base of the tin, then grease the paper, taking care not to move the side strips.

Lining a square tin

Lining a round tin

ROUND TIN

1 Put the tin on a sheet of greaseproof paper and draw a circle around its circumference. Cut out the circle just inside the drawn line.

2 Cut a strip or strips about 2cm (¾ inch) wider than the depth of the tin and fold up one long edge of each strip by 1cm (½ inch). Make cuts, about 2.5cm (1 inch) apart, through the folded edge of the strip(s) up to the fold line.

3 Lightly grease the tin with butter, making sure it is completely coated.

4 Press the strip(s) on to the sides of the tin so that the snipped edge sits on the base.

5 Lay the circle in the bottom of the tin and grease the paper.

SWISS ROLL TIN

Use this method for a Swiss roll or any other shallow baking tin.

1 Lightly grease the tin with butter, making sure it is completely coated.

2 Cut a piece of baking parchment into a rectangle 7.5cm (3 inch) wider and longer than the tin. Press it into the tin and cut at the corners, then fold to fit neatly. Grease all over.

LOAF TIN

1 Lightly grease the tin with butter, making sure it is completely coated.

2 Cut out a sheet of greaseproof paper to the same length as the base and wide enough to cover both the base and the long sides. Press it into position, making sure that it sits snugly in the corners.

3 Now cut another sheet to the same width as the base and long enough to cover both the base and the ends of the tin. Press into place. Grease the paper all over.

SHAPED TINS

• Round and square are the traditional shapes for cake tins, but tins come in many different shapes, including numerals, and can be either purchased or hired from cake decorating shops. The advantage of these tins is that they give more scope for matching the cake to the occasion.

• To line a shaped tin, follow the instructions for a round tin, above.

Lining a loaf tin

Making roulades

LINERS

Reusable, non-stick, silicone baking mats and liners are widely available and, as there is no need to grease them, they reduce the fat in your baking. Look out also for silicone muffin trays and cupcake moulds.

MAKING ROULADES

A roulade is made from a very light cake mixture and does not contain flour. It remains very soft when baked, and can therefore be easily rolled around a layer of filling such as jam and cream (see Black Forest Roulade, page 40).

MAKING CUPCAKES AND MUFFINS

Cupcakes and muffins are two members of the same family: individual cakes, usually based on a mixture made with self-raising flour, baked in bun tins or muffin pans, so that it rises and sets to an airy texture (see pages 58–79). The secret to really light, fluffy muffins is a light hand. Be sure to sift the flour and stir the mixture as little as possible; it's ok if it looks a little lumpy. Over-mixing will give tough, chewy results.

MAKING CHEESECAKES

A cheesecake is more of a deep tart than a cake. It is essentially a rich flavoured mixture of eggs, cream and full- or low-fat soft cheese, curd cheese or cottage cheese – set on a buttery biscuit, sponge or pastry base. Cheesecakes are either baked to cook and set the filling, or uncooked and set with gelatine. Use a spring-release cake tin to make the cake easier to unmould.

When baking cheeesecakes, watch the temperature – too high a heat can cause the top to crack (see page 309).

The mixture for an uncooked cheesecake is poured on to a biscuit crumb base that has been pressed into a flan tin, then chilled until firm. The whole cheesecake is then chilled to set.

Making cupcakes and muffins   *Making cheesecakes*

BAKING THE CAKE

Bake the cake mixture as soon as you have made it, as the raising agents will start to react straight away. Once the cake is in the oven, resist the temptation to open the door – a sudden gush of cold air will make a part-baked cake sink. Instead, wait until the cooking time is almost up before testing. If your cake appears to be browning too quickly, cover the top loosely with greaseproof paper towards the end of cooking.

Apart from very light sponges, all cakes are best left to stand in their tin for 5–10 minutes after baking to firm up slightly.

TESTING CAKES

Ovens vary and the time given in the recipe might be too short or too long to correctly cook what you are baking. So always test to ensure a successful result.

TESTING SPONGES

1 Gently press the centre of the sponge. It should feel springy. If it's a whisked cake, it should be just shrinking away from the sides of the tin.
2 If you have to put it back into the oven, close the door gently so that the vibrations don't cause the cake to sink in the centre.

TESTING FRUIT CAKES

1 To test if a fruit cake is cooked, insert a skewer into the centre of the cake, leave for a few moments, then pull it out. If it comes away clean, the cake is ready.
2 If any mixture sticks to the skewer, the cake is not quite done, so put the cake back in the oven for a few more minutes, then test again with a clean skewer.

Testing sponges

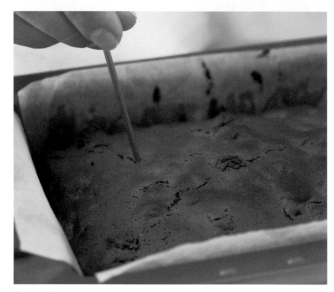

Testing fruit cakes

COOLING CAKES

- Sponge cakes should be taken out of their tins soon after baking. Invert on to a wire rack lined with sugar-dusted baking parchment.

- Leave fruit cakes to cool in the tin for 15 minutes before turning out.

- Allow rich fruit cakes to cool completely before turning out; there is a risk of breaking otherwise.

STORING CAKES

With the exception of rich fruit cakes and gingerbread, most cakes are best enjoyed freshly baked. If storing is necessary, use a cake tin or large plastic container. Make sure that the cake is completely cold before you put it into the container. If you haven't a large enough container, wrap the cake in a double layer of greaseproof paper and overwrap with foil. Avoid putting rich fruit cakes in direct contact with foil – the fruit may react with it. Never store a cake in the same tin as biscuits, as the biscuits will quickly soften.

Most cakes, particularly sponges, freeze well, but they are generally best frozen before filling and decorating. If freezing a finished gâteau, open-freeze first, then pack in a rigid container.

Successful biscuit-making

As with cake-making, the key to successful biscuit-making is to accurately weigh the ingredients and follow the recipe carefully. See also page 311.

METHODS

The main techniques in biscuit making are: creaming (Chocolate Chip Oat Cookies, page 97), the all-in-one method (Hazelnut and Chocolate Biscotti, page 108), rolled (Christmas Cookies, page 102), refrigerator biscuits (Refrigerator Cake, page 124 – form the mixture into a roll, chill until firm, then cut into slices), whisked (Orange Tuile Biscuits, page 104), melted (Ginger Biscuits, page 98), moulded (The Ultimate Chocolate Chip Cookie, page 98), and piped (Amaretti Biscuits, page 105).

BAKING SHEETS

Use a shiny-based baking sheet; a darker-coloured sheet will absorb a greater amount of heat and can therefore burn the undersides of the biscuits.

BAKING BISCUITS

For hints on baking the perfect biscuits and cookies, see page 311. Once baked, biscuits, with their high sugar content, will seem very soft. They should be left on the baking sheet for a few minutes before transferring to a wire rack.

STORING BISCUITS

Most biscuits are best enjoyed freshly baked. However, if storing, never put in the same tin as a cake, and preferably not with other types of biscuits, as they quickly soften and absorb other flavours.

CRUSHING BISCUITS FOR CHEESECAKE BASES

Crush the biscuits to a fine powder in a food processor. (Alternatively, put them into a plastic bag and crush with a rolling pin.)

FILLING BISCUITS

Cream filling:
To sandwich about 18 biscuits, cream 50g (2oz) butter until soft, then beat in 75g (3oz) sifted icing sugar. Mix well and soften by adding a few drops of orange juice or vanilla extract until the mixture is of a firm, spreadable consistency. Spread the mixture on to the flat side of a biscuit and gently press a second biscuit on top to make a sandwich.

Chocolate filling:
To fill about 18 biscuits, cream 50g (2oz) butter until soft, then add 75g (3oz) icing sugar and 2 tsp cocoa powder. Mix well and add a few drops of milk to soften if necessary.

Toffee filling:
Spread dulce de leche over one biscuit and top with another. Roll the edges in desiccated coconut, if you like.

Filling biscuits

HOW TO MAKE PERFECT CAKES

- Weigh out all the ingredients carefully before starting the recipe, so that you have everything to hand when you begin to make the cake.

- Always work in metric or imperial – never mix the two measurements.

- Check that you have the correct cake tin for the job. The tin sizes quoted in this book refer to the base measurement of the tin.

- Always line the tin properly where necessary.

- Allow the oven to preheat to the correct temperature.

- Try not to be heavy-handed – when folding in flour, use light strokes so the air doesn't get knocked out.

- Don't let a cake mixture sit around once you've made it: pop it straight into the cake tin and into the oven, otherwise the raising agents will start to react.

- After it has come out of the oven, leave the cake in the tin to cool for 10 minutes and then turn out on to a wire rack to cool completely.

- Let the tins cool completely before washing them in warm, soapy water with a non-abrasive sponge.

WHAT WENT WRONG?

THE CAKE SINKS IN THE MIDDLE
- The oven door was opened too soon.

- The cake was under-baked.

- The ingredients haven't been measured accurately.

- The wrong size cake tin may have been used.

THE CAKE HAS A CRACKED, DOMED TOP
- The oven temperature was too hot.

- The cake was too near the top of the oven.

- Insufficient liquid was used.

- The baking tin was too small.

- Too much raising agent was used.

THE CAKE HAS A DENSE TEXTURE
- The mixture curdled when adding the eggs.

- Too much liquid was used.

- The mixture was over-folded.

- Too little raising agent was used or an ineffective raising agent that is past its 'use-by date' was used.

THE FRUIT HAS SUNK TO THE BOTTOM
- The mixture was too soft to support the weight of the fruit. This is liable to happen if the fruit was too sticky or wet.

THE CAKE EDGES ARE CRUNCHY
- The baking tin was over-greased.

HOW TO MAKE PERFECT CHEESECAKES

- When making cheesecakes, bring eggs and cream cheese to room temperature before using.

- Use good-quality cream cheese for the best results.

- Cream cheese will give richer-tasting cheesecakes.

WHAT WENT WRONG?

THE CHEESECAKE IS DRY
- The cheesecake was over-baked.

CRACK IN THE SURFACE OF THE CHEESECAKE
- The cheesecake was over-baked.

- The cheesecake was cooled too quickly – leave to cool in a switched-off oven with the door ajar.

THE CHEESECAKE CENTRE IS STILL RUNNY
- The cheesecake was under-cooked.

- The oven temperature was too low.

THE CHEESECAKE IS GRAINY IN TEXTURE
- The cheesecake was over-baked.

- The oven temperature was too high.

ICING AND DECORATING

FILLING AND TOPPING CAKES

To make sponge cakes even tastier, they can be split and filled with jam, cream or buttercream. Icings complete a special-occasion cake and are especially good when covering home-made almond paste.

SPLITTING AND FILLING A CAKE

1 Leave the cake to cool completely before splitting. Use a knife with a shallow thin blade, such as a bread knife, a ham knife, or a carving knife. Cut a notch from top to bottom on one side so you will know where to line the pieces up.

2 Cut midway between top and bottom, about one-third of the way through the cake. Turn the cake while cutting, taking care to keep the blade parallel with the base, until you have cut all the way around.

3 Cut through the central core and lift off the top of the cake.

4 Warm the filling slightly to make it easier to spread, then spread on top of the base, stopping 1cm (½ inch) from the edge. Add the top layer of cake.

BASIC ICINGS AND FROSTINGS

There are lots of options for covering cakes, depending on the finish you require. Royal and glacé icings are the classics. Almond paste, followed by a layer of ready-to-roll icing (sugar paste) is popular, as is buttercream or apricot glaze.

GLACÉ ICING

To make 225g (8oz), enough to cover 18 fairy cakes, you will need: 225g (8oz) icing sugar, a few drops of vanilla or almond flavouring (optional), 2–3 tbsp boiling water, food colouring (optional).

1 Sift the icing sugar into a bowl. Add a few drops of flavouring, if you like.

2 Using a wooden spoon, gradually stir in enough water until the mixture is the consistency of thick cream. Beat until white and smooth and the icing is thick enough to coat the back of the spoon. Add colouring, if you like, and use immediately.

VARIATIONS

- **Orange or lemon:** Replace the water with strained orange or lemon juice.
- **Chocolate:** Sift 2 tsp cocoa powder with the icing sugar.
- **Colour:** Add a few drops of liquid food colouring, or use food colouring paste for a stronger colour.

NOTE

Food colourings are available in liquid, paste or powder form. Add minute amounts with the tip of a cocktail stick until the desired colour is achieved.

Splitting and filling a cake

ROYAL ICING

Royal icing can also be bought in packs from supermarkets. Simply add water or egg white to use.

To make 450g (1lb), enough to cover the top and sides of a 20.5cm (8 inch) cake, you will need:
2 medium egg whites, ¼ tsp lemon juice, 450g (1lb) icing sugar, sifted, 1 tsp glycerine.

1 Put the egg whites and lemon juice into a clean bowl. Stir to break up the egg whites. Add sufficient icing sugar to mix to the consistency of unwhipped cream. Continue mixing and adding small quantities of icing sugar until the desired consistency is reached, mixing well and gently beating after each addition. The icing should be smooth, glossy and light, almost like a cold meringue in texture, but not aerated. Do not add the icing sugar too quickly or it will produce a dull heavy icing. Stir in the glycerine until well blended. (Alternatively, for large quantities of royal icing, use a food mixer on the lowest speed, following the same instructions as before.)
2 Allow the icing to settle before using it; cover the surface with a piece of damp clingfilm and seal well, excluding all the air.
3 Stir the icing thoroughly before use to disperse any air bubbles, then adjust the consistency if necessary by adding more sifted icing sugar.

APRICOT GLAZE

To make 450g (1lb), you will need:
450g (1lb) apricot jam, 2 tbsp water.

1 Put the jam and water into a saucepan and heat gently, stirring occasionally, until melted. Boil the jam rapidly for 1 minute, then strain through a sieve.
2 Using a wooden spoon, rub through as much fruit as possible. Discard the skins left in the sieve.
3 Pour the glaze into a clean, hot jar, then seal with a clean lid and cool. Store in the fridge for up to two months. You only need 3–4 tbsp apricot glaze for a 23cm (9 inch) cake, so this quantity will glaze 6–7 cakes.

ALMOND PASTE

To make 450g (1lb) almond paste, enough to cover the top and sides of an 18cm (7 inch) round cake or 15cm (6 inch) square cake, you will need:
225g (8oz) ground almonds, 125g (4oz) golden caster sugar, 125g (4oz) sifted golden icing sugar, 1 large egg, 2 tsp lemon juice, 1 tsp sherry, 1–2 drops vanilla extract.

1 Put the ground almonds and sugars into a bowl and stir to combine. In another bowl, whisk together the remaining ingredients, then add to the dry ingredients.
2 Stir well to mix, pounding gently to release some of the oil from the almonds. Knead with your hands until smooth, then cover until ready to use.

NOTE

If you wish to avoid using raw egg to bind the almond paste, mix the other liquid ingredients with a little water instead.

FONDANT ICING

To make 500g (1lb 2oz), enough to cover the top and sides of an 18cm (7 inch) round cake or 15cm (6 inch) square cake, you will need:
500g (1lb 2oz) golden icing sugar, plus extra to dust, 1 medium egg white, 2 tbsp liquid glucose, warmed, 1 tsp vanilla extract.

Whiz the icing sugar in a food processor for 30 seconds, then add the egg white, glucose and vanilla extract and whiz for 2–3 minutes until the mixture forms a ball.

VANILLA FROSTING

To make about 175g (6oz), enough to cover the top and sides of an 18cm (7 inch) cake, you will need:
150g (5oz) icing sugar, 5 tsp vegetable oil, 1 tbsp milk, a few drops of vanilla extract.

Sift the icing sugar into a bowl and, using a wooden spoon, beat in the oil, milk and vanilla extract until smooth.

COFFEE FUDGE FROSTING

To make 400g (14oz), enough to cover the top and sides of a 20.5cm (8 inch) cake, you will need:

50g (2oz) unsalted butter, 125g (4oz) light muscovado sugar, 2 tbsp single cream or milk, 1 tbsp coffee granules, 200g (7oz) golden icing sugar, sifted.

1 Put the butter, muscovado sugar and cream or milk into a pan. Dissolve the coffee in 2 tbsp boiling water and add to the pan. Heat gently until the sugar dissolves, then bring to the boil and boil briskly for 3 minutes.

2 Remove from the heat and gradually stir in the icing sugar. Beat well with a wooden spoon for 1 minute until smooth.

3 Use the frosting immediately, spreading it over the cake with a wet palette knife, or dilute with a little water to use as a smooth coating.

VARIATION

Chocolate fudge frosting: Omit the coffee. Add 75g (3oz) plain chocolate, in pieces, to the pan with the butter at the beginning of step 1.

AMERICAN FROSTING

To make 225g (8oz), enough to cover the top and sides of a 20.5cm (8 inch) cake, you will need:

1 large egg white, 225g (8oz) golden caster or granulated sugar, pinch of cream of tartar.

1 Whisk the egg white in a clean bowl until stiff. Put the sugar, 4 tbsp water and the cream of tartar into a heavy-based pan. Heat gently, stirring, until the sugar has dissolved. Bring to the boil, without stirring, and boil until the sugar syrup registers 115°C on a sugar thermometer.

2 Remove from the heat and, as soon as the bubbles subside, pour the syrup on to the egg white in a thin stream, whisking constantly until thick and white. Leave to cool slightly.

3 When the frosting begins to turn dull around the edges and is almost cold, pour quickly over the cake and spread evenly with a palette knife.

SEVEN-MINUTE FROSTING

To make about 175g (6oz), enough to cover the top and sides of an 18cm (7 inch) cake, you will need:

1 medium egg white, 175g (6oz) caster sugar, 2 tbsp water, pinch of salt, pinch of cream of tartar.

1 Put all the ingredients into a heatproof bowl and whisk lightly using an electric or hand whisk.

2 Put the bowl over a pan of hot water, making sure the base of the bowl doesn't touch the water, and heat, whisking continuously, until the mixture thickens sufficiently to stand in peaks. This will take about 7 minutes.

3 Pour the frosting over the top of the cake and spread with a palette knife.

BUTTERCREAM

To cover the top of a 20.5cm (8 inch) cake, you will need:

75g (3oz) unsalted butter, 175g (6oz) icing sugar, sifted, a few drops of vanilla extract, 1–2 tbsp milk.

1 Soften the butter in a mixing bowl, then beat until light and fluffy.

2 Gradually stir in the remaining ingredients and beat until smooth.

VARIATIONS

- **Citrus:** Replace the vanilla with a little grated orange, lemon or lime zest, and use some of the fruit's juice in place of the milk.
- **Chocolate:** Blend 1 tbsp cocoa powder with 2 tbsp boiling water. Cool, then add to the mixture in place of the milk.
- **Colour:** For a strong colour, use food colouring paste; liquid colouring gives a paler effect.

EASIEST ICING

To make 675g (1½lb), enough to cover a 20.5cm (8 inch) almond paste-covered cake, you will need:

3 medium egg whites, 2 tbsp lemon juice, 2 tsp glycerine, 675g (1½lb) icing sugar, sifted.

1 Put the egg whites into a large bowl and whisk until frothy. There should be just a layer of bubbles across the top. Add the lemon juice, glycerine and 2 tbsp icing sugar and whisk until smooth.

2 Whisk in the rest of the sugar, a little at a time, until the mixture is smooth, thick and forming soft peaks.

3 Using a palette knife, smooth half the icing over the top and sides of the cake, then repeat using the remaining icing to cover. Run the knife around the sides to neaten, then use the tip to make peaks all over the top. Leave to dry in a cool place for at least 48 hours.

CHOCOLATE GANACHE

To make 225g (8oz), enough to cover an 18cm (7 inch) round cake, you will need: 225g (8oz) good-quality plain dark chocolate (with 60–70 per cent cocoa solids), chopped into small pieces, 250ml (9fl oz) double cream.

1 Put the chocolate into a medium heatproof bowl. Pour the cream into a small heavy-based pan and bring to the boil.
2 Immediately pour the cream on to the chocolate and stir gently in one direction until the chocolate has melted and the mixture is smooth. Set aside to cool for 5 minutes.
3 Whisk the ganache until it begins to hold its shape. Used at room temperature, the mixture should be the consistency of softened butter.

NOTE
Use ganache at room temperature as a smooth coating for special cakes, or chill it lightly until thickened and use to fill meringues, choux buns or sandwich cakes.

VARIATIONS
These are all suitable for a sauce made with 225g (8oz) chocolate:
- **Milk or single cream:** Substituted in whole or in part for the water.
- **Coffee:** Stir in 1 tsp instant coffee or a shot of espresso when melting the chocolate.
- **Spices:** Add a pinch of ground cinnamon, crushed cardamom seeds or freshly grated nutmeg to the melting chocolate.
- **Vanilla extract:** Stir in ¼ tsp vanilla when melting the chocolate.
- **Rum, whisky or Cognac:** Stir in about 1 tsp alcohol when melting the chocolate.
- **Butter:** Stir in 25g (1oz) towards the end of heating.

Baking bread is one of the greatest pleasures of the kitchen, and one of the simplest. Simple loaves provide the foundation for further experimentation, so they are the best place to start with bread-making (see White Farmhouse Loaf, page 214). See also pages 320–21.

INGREDIENTS

The basic ingredients for bread-making are very simple, but you can also experiment with flavourings. Savoury doughs can be enhanced with cheese, fresh herbs, olives or sun-dried tomatoes, for example; while sweet doughs are enriched with dried fruits, nuts, vanilla sugar, or scented spices like cinnamon and nutmeg.

YEAST Yeast is available in a number of different forms, which are interchangeable in recipes providing that the method is adjusted accordingly. As a rough guide, 15g (½oz) fresh yeast, a 7g sachet (2 tsp) fast-action (easy-blend) dried yeast, or 1 tbsp ordinary dried yeast is enough to rise 700g (1½lb) flour. In general, if you add more than this, the dough will not rise any higher and the bread is likely to have an unpleasant yeasty taste. However, if the dough is enriched with fruit, sugar, butter or nuts, the rise is more difficult and you will usually need more yeast – be guided by the recipes.
Fast-action dried yeast, also called easy-blend dried yeast, is now the most readily available dried form. It is sprinkled directly into the flour and the liquid is mixed in afterwards. After kneading, the dough can be shaped straightaway and only requires one rising. However, for enriched doughs – particularly heavily fruited ones – better results are obtained if the dough is given the traditional two rises. Always make sure you adhere to the 'use-by' date on the pack; fast-action dried yeast won't work if it is stale. **Traditional dried yeast** needs sugar to activate it. If using milk as the liquid, the natural sugars present in the milk will be enough; if using water, you will need to add a pinch of sugar. To use traditional dried yeast, blend it with the warm liquid (see opposite), adding a pinch of sugar if needed, and leave it in a warm place for about 15 minutes until a frothy head develops. This shows that the yeast is active. If it refuses to froth, then it is probably past its 'use-by date'; discard and begin again with a fresh pack of yeast. **Fresh yeast** is a living organism and must be handled in the right way in order to work effectively. It is available from some healthfood shops, bakers and supermarkets. It should be firm, moist and creamy coloured with a good 'yeasty' smell. If it is dry and crumbly with brown patches, it is probably stale and won't work effectively. When you buy fresh yeast it is alive, but inactive. Only when it is mixed with a warm liquid does it become active and release the gases that make the dough rise. Fresh yeast is easy to use: simply blend with a little of the liquid specified in the recipe, add the remaining liquid, then mix into the flour. Fresh yeast will stay fresh for about three days if stored in the fridge, or it can be frozen for up to three months.

Leaving the dough to rise

Sourdough starter is a traditional method that has regained popularity. A mixture of yeast, flour and water is left to ferment for several days and then added to the dough. A sourdough starter produces a close-textured loaf with a distinctive flavour. If you make bread regularly, a sourdough starter is a convenient way of leavening. Simply blend 15g (½oz) fresh yeast (or 1 tsp dried yeast) with 450ml (¾ pint) warm water and about 225g (8oz) strong plain white flour or enough to make a thick pourable batter. Cover the bowl with a damp cloth and leave at room temperature for 3–5 days to ferment and develop the sourdough flavour. Use 125ml (4fl oz) starter to replace each 15g (½oz) fresh yeast called for in a recipe, then make the bread in the usual way. To store, keep it in the fridge and use within 1 week. Sourdough starter keeps well but must be 'refreshed'. Keep the starter covered in the fridge and whisk in a handful of flour and a small cup of water every day – this provides fresh nutrients for the yeast and aids its leavening properties.

LIQUID No matter which variety of yeast you are using, the liquid should be just warm or tepid, that is at a temperature of 43°C, which will feel slightly warm to the fingertips. If it is too hot it could kill the yeast; if too cold the yeast will not begin to work. **Milk** gives bread a slightly softer texture than water. You should always regard any quantity of liquid specified in a recipe as a guide because flour absorbency varies according to the type of flour, and from brand to brand.

FLOUR Various flours are used for bread-making. **Strong flours** give better results because they have a higher proportion of protein, which helps the formation of gluten – the substance that stretches the dough and traps in air as it cooks, to give bread its characteristic airy texture. **Ordinary plain flour** produces a close-textured crumbly loaf. **Strong white bread flour** is ideal. If possible, use unbleached white flour, which has not been chemically treated to whiten it. **Strong wholemeal bread flour** is ground from the whole wheat kernel and has a coarser texture than white flour, with a fuller flavour and more nutrients; it is also an excellent source of fibre. This flour lends a distinctive flavour, but it is best used with some strong white flour to obtain a good textured loaf. Bread made with 100% wholemeal flour has a heavy, dense texture. **Strong brown bread flour** has a percentage of the bran removed and therefore has a finer texture than wholemeal flour. **Stoneground flour** takes its name from the specific grinding process – between stones – which heats the flour and gives it a slightly roasted, nutty flavour. Both stoneground wholemeal and brown flours are available. **Granary flour** is a strong brown flour, with added malted wheat flakes, which give it a distinctive flavour. **Rye flour** makes a dark, close-textured bread with plenty of flavour. As it is low in gluten, it must be mixed with a strong white flour for best results.

SALT An important ingredient in breads because it controls fermentation, strengthens gluten and improves the flavour. However, it also slows down the action of yeast, so don't add too much. Be guided by the amount specified in the recipe.

FAT Some recipes call for a little fat to be rubbed into the flour before the yeast is added. This improves the keeping quality of the bread and imparts extra flavour, but too much fat will slow down the action of the yeast.

MIXING AND KNEADING THE DOUGH

Some recipes recommend warming the flour and mixing bowl in advance. If using fresh or 'ordinary' dried yeast, or if you are working in a cold room, this helps to speed things up a little, but otherwise it isn't necessary.

After mixing the yeast and liquid into the dry ingredients, vigorous kneading is required to strengthen the gluten in the flour, make the dough elastic and ultimately to achieve a good rise. If you omit this stage, the dough will not rise. There is nothing difficult about kneading and, contrary to popular belief, it doesn't take long – 10 minutes should be enough. Turn the dough on to a floured surface, fold it firmly towards you, then quickly and firmly push it down and away from you with the heel of your hand. Give it a quarter turn and continue kneading until the dough feels elastic and smooth: it shouldn't be sticky. As an alternative to kneading by hand, you can use a large mixer with a dough hook attachment.

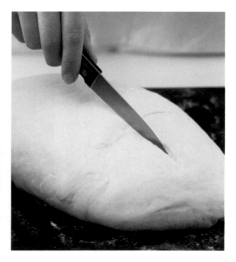

Mixing and kneading the dough

HOW TO MAKE PERFECT BREAD

- Make sure shaped dough has risen sufficiently – usually to double.

- Always oil or flour the loaf tin, or baking sheet, to prevent sticking.

- Make sure the oven is at the correct temperature before baking.

- Bake on a preheated ceramic baking stone (from good kitchen shops) if possible, even if the bread is in a loaf tin. The heat of the stone will give the bread a crisp base.

- If baked bread is left for too long either in the loaf tin or on the baking sheet, steam will gather and, as a result, the underneath will start to become soggy. To prevent this, always remove the loaf immediately and put it on a wire rack. Then leave it to cool completely before slicing, as you like.

WHAT WENT WRONG?

THE LOAF HASN'T RISEN PROPERLY
- Not enough liquid was added during mixing.

- Too much salt or sugar was added during mixing.

- The yeast was stale.

- The liquid was too hot and killed the yeast.

- The second proving wasn't long enough.

- The second proving was too long causing it to collapse during baking.

THE BREAD IS CAKE-LIKE OR OVER-DENSE
- The dough wasn't kneaded for long enough.

- The dough was under-proved.

- Too much salt was added.

- Too much fat was added.

- Not enough, or too little, liquid was added.

THE BREAD HAS HOLES IN IT
- The dough wasn't knocked back sufficiently.

- The dough was over-proved.

THE BREAD HAS A CRACKED CRUST
- The oven was too hot.

- The dough was under-proved.

DOS AND DON'TS OF MACHINE-BAKED BREAD

- Use recipes that have been designed for bread machine use only, as conventional bread recipes use different quantities of ingredients and are not converted easily.

- Measure out all the ingredients carefully, as exact quantities are essential for a perfect loaf.

- Always follow the bread machine instructions carefully; it is essential that the ingredients go into the machine in the order stated, as the yeast must not come into contact with the liquid until the machine begins to mix.

- Avoid lifting the lid during the rising and baking cycles, as this may cause the loaf to sink.

- The loaf is best removed from the machine as soon as it is baked, otherwise it will become soggy.

PASTRY-MAKING TECHNIQUES

The art of making good pastry lies in paying careful attention to the recipe and using the correct proportion of fat to flour. It is important to 'rest' pastry before baking, as it gets stretched during shaping and if not allowed to 'rest' and firm up, it may shrink away from the sides of the tin during baking.

INGREDIENTS

FLOUR For most pastries, **plain flour** works best, as it gives a light, crisp result. Self-raising flour would produce a soft spongy pastry. Wholemeal flour gives a heavier dough, which is more difficult to roll. For wholemeal pastry, it is therefore preferable to use half wholemeal and half white flour. Puff pastry is usually made with strong plain (bread) flour as this contains extra gluten to strengthen the dough, enabling it to withstand intensive rolling and folding. A little lemon juice is usually added to puff pastry to soften the gluten and make the dough more elastic.

FAT Traditionally, shortcrust pastry is made with a mixture of **lard** (for shortness) and **either butter or margarine** (for flavour). However, it is now more often made with a mixture of **white vegetable fat** and butter or margarine, or all butter for a rich flavour. If margarine is preferred, it should be the hard, block type rather than soft-tub margarine.

LIQUID Care must be taken when adding the liquid to a pastry dough: too much will result in a tough end result; too little will produce a crumbly pastry, which is difficult to handle. Use **chilled water** and add just enough to bind the dough. **Egg yolks** are often used to enrich pastry.

QUANTITIES

Tart tins vary in depth, which affects the quantity of pastry needed. The following quantities are approximate.

Tart tin size	Pastry
18cm (7 inch)	125g (4oz)
20.5cm (8 inch)	175g (6oz)
23cm (9 inch)	200g (7oz)
25.5cm (10 inch)	225g (8oz)

USING PASTRY

A light touch and a little care with rolling and lifting your prepared dough will ensure your pastry case or pie crust is crisp and perfect. Take your time for the best results.

LINING TART AND PIE TINS

1 Working carefully, roll out chilled dough on a floured surface to make a sheet at least 5cm (2 inch) larger than the tart tin or pie dish. Roll the dough on to the rolling pin, then unroll it on to the tin, covering it completely with an even overhang all round. Don't stretch the dough.

2 Lift the hanging dough with one hand while you press it gently but firmly into the base and sides of the tin. Don't stretch the dough while you're pressing it down.

3 For a tart case, roll the rolling pin over the tin and remove the excess dough for later use. For a pie dish, ensure the pastry covers the lip of the dish.

4 Push the dough into and up the sides of the tin or dish, so that the dough rises a little over the edge.

Lining tart tins and pie dishes

BAKING BLIND

Cooking the pastry before filling gives a crisp result.

1 Preheat the oven according to the recipe. Prick the pastry base with a fork. Cover with foil or greaseproof paper 8cm (3¼ inch) larger than the tin.

2 Spread baking beans on top. Bake for 15 minutes. Remove the foil or paper and beans and bake for 5–10 minutes until light golden.

TOPPING

Covered pies need a lid of equal thickness to the base.

1 Roll out the pastry on a floured surface to about 2.5cm (1 inch) larger than the baking tin or dish. Roll on to the rolling pin, then unroll over the pie with an even overhang.

2 Using a small knife, cut off the overhang just outside the rim.

SEALING

1 Using your thumb and index finger, pinch the base and top of the pastry dough all the way round the rim. You don't need to squeeze hard, just firmly enough to stick them together. If the pie has no base, just press the top down on the rim of the tin or dish.

2 Use a fork to make decorative fluting marks on the rim – simply press all around the edge of the pie with the back of a floured fork. (See also below.)

FINISHING

1 If you want to make decorations for the pie using leftover pastry, cut them out using pastry cutters and put them in place, using a little water to stick them to the pastry. For pastry leaves, cut neat strips from the pastry trimmings, then cut these on the diagonal into diamonds, to shape leaves. Use the back of the knife to mark veins and pinch one end to form a stem.

2 Brush the top of the pastry with beaten egg if you wish. Cut two slits in the top of the pie using a small, sharp knife to let the steam escape during baking.

Baking blind

Topping

Sealing

Finishing

DOS AND DON'TS OF PASTRY-MAKING

HOW TO MAKE PERFECT SHORTCRUST, PÂTE SUCRÉE AND PUFF PASTRY

- Work in a cool kitchen.

- Always use chilled water and butter whenever specified.

- It helps to chill the bowl too, if your hands are very warm.

- Use good-quality butter for tastier pastry.

- Use your fingertips when rubbing in.

- Avoid over-handling the pastry or it will become heavy.

- Don't over-flour the worksurface, as it will make your pastry too dry.

- Allow pastry to relax for easier rolling out.

- To stop it collapsing, chill the pastry well before putting in the oven.

SHORTCRUST PASTRY – WHAT WENT WRONG?

THE TART EDGES ARE UNEVEN/SHRUNKEN
- It wasn't chilled thoroughly before baking.

- Too much water was added at the mixing stage.

- The oven temperature wasn't hot enough.

- The pastry was over-stretched when rolling and lining.

THE PASTRY IS TOUGH
- The fat wasn't rubbed in properly.

- Too little fat.

- Too much water was added during mixing.

- The pastry was kneaded too much, which over-developed the gluten.

THE PASTRY IS SOFT AND CRUMBLY
- Too much fat was added.

- Too little water was added.

THE PASTRY HAS BLISTERED
- The fat wasn't rubbed in properly.

- Too much water was added.

THE PASTRY IS GREASY
- It was overcooked.

- It was overworked.

PÂTE SUCRÉE – WHAT WENT WRONG?

THE PASTRY IS TOUGH
- The pastry was overworked when the dough was brought together.

- The pastry was overcooked.

THE PASTRY IS OILY
- The butter was too warm.

PUFF PASTRY – WHAT WENT WRONG?

THE PASTRY HASN'T RISEN
- The butter broke through the pastry when rolled.

- The pastry was rolled and folded too many times.

THE PASTRY ISN'T FLAKY
- Butter not cool enough when used.

- Insufficient resting and chilling.

- Over-heavy rolling.

FAT HAS RUN OUT DURING BAKING
- The oven was too cool.

- The ends of the pastry were not sealed.

THE PASTRY IS OILY
- The pastry was over-baked.

- The pastry was not properly chilled.

THE PASTRY IS TOUGH
- Too much water was added at the first stage.

HOW TO MAKE PERFECT CHOUX PASTRY

This soft pastry is usually spooned or piped and is excellent for making cream-filled buns, profiteroles and savouries. It contains a lot of water and so it puffs up beautifully and is wonderfully light and airy.

- Before you start, have all the ingredients carefully measured and in place.

- Tip in all the flour at once, then leave the mixture to cool before beating in the eggs gradually.

- Use a dampened baking sheet (the steam will help the pastry to rise), and don't open the oven door for the first 20 minutes of baking, as the cold air will make the pastry sink.

CHOUX PASTRY – WHAT WENT WRONG?

THE MIXTURE IS TOO SOFT
- Insufficient cooking of flour before adding the egg.

- Insufficient beating after addition of egg.

THE PASTRY HASN'T RISE ENOUGH DURING BAKING
- Not enough egg was beaten into the mixture.

- The mixture was too warm when the egg was added.

- The oven was too cool.

- The mixture was under-cooked.

- The mixture wasn't beaten enough.

- The oven door was opened before the pastry had set.

THE PASTRY HAS SUNK
- Insufficient baking, which can sometimes be remedied by returning the pastry to the oven.

HOW TO WORK WITH FILO PASTRY

Making filo pastry is time-consuming, but ready-made filo is an excellent alternative. The delicate sheets of pastry are usually brushed with butter, then layered and filled to create crisp, golden treats.

- Filo pastry is often sold frozen; if you plan to put it into the freezer at home, get it home quickly so that it doesn't thaw.

- Thaw it completely before you start to work with it, otherwise it can crack or crumble. The best way to do this is to leave it to thaw overnight in the fridge.

- As you work, cover the unused sheets with a clean damp teatowel, to prevent them from drying out.

FILO PASTRY – WHAT WENT WRONG?

THE PASTRY CRACKS WHEN ROLLED
- The pastry became too dry. Brush with oil or melted butter. Keep the rest of the pastry covered with a damp teatowel while assembling.

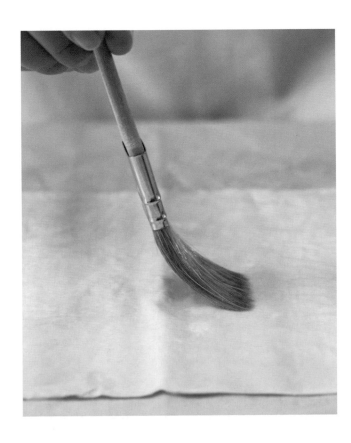

VANILLA ICE CREAM

To serve four to six, you will need:
300ml (½ pint) full-fat milk, I vanilla pod, split lengthways,
3 medium egg yolks, 75g (3oz) golden caster sugar; 300ml (½ pint)
double cream.

1 Put the milk and vanilla pod into a pan. Heat slowly until
almost boiling. Cool for 20 minutes, then remove the vanilla pod.
Whisk the egg yolks and sugar together in a large bowl until thick
and creamy. Gradually whisk in the milk, then strain back into the
pan.

2 Cook over a low heat, stirring with a wooden spoon, until thick
enough to coat the back of the spoon – do not boil. Pour into a
chilled bowl and leave to cool.

3 Whisk the cream into the custard. Pour into an ice-cream
maker and freeze or churn according to the manufacturer's
instructions or make by hand (see below). Store in a covered
freezerproof container for up to two months. Put the ice cream in
the fridge for 15–20 minutes before serving to soften slightly.

VARIATIONS

* **Fruit Ice Cream:** Sweeten 300ml (½ pint) fruit purée (such as
  rhubarb, gooseberry, raspberry or strawberry) to taste, then
  stir into the cooked custard and churn.
* **Chocolate Ice Cream:** Omit the vanilla and add 125g (4oz)
  plain chocolate to the milk. Heat gently until melted, then bring
  almost to the boil and proceed as above.
* **Coffee Ice Cream:** Omit the vanilla and add 150ml (¼ pint)
  cooled strong coffee to the cooked custard.

MAKING ICE CREAM BY HAND

1 If possible, set the freezer to fast freeze I hour ahead. Pour the
ice cream mixture into a shallow freezerproof container, cover and
freeze until partially frozen.

2 Spoon into a bowl and mash with a fork to break up the ice
crystals. Return to the container and freeze for a further 2 hours.
Repeat and freeze for another 3 hours.

VANILLA CUSTARD

To serve eight, you will need:
600ml (I pint) full-fat milk, I vanilla pod or I tbsp vanilla extract,
6 large egg yolks, 2 tbsp golden caster sugar, 2 tbsp cornflour.

1 Put the milk into a pan. Split the vanilla pod and scrape the
seeds into the pan, then drop in the pod. If using vanilla extract,
pour it in. Bring to the boil, then turn off the heat and leave to
cool for 5 minutes.

2 Put the egg yolks, sugar and cornflour into a bowl and whisk to
blend. Remove the vanilla pod from the milk and gradually whisk
the warm milk into the egg mixture.

3 Rinse out the pan. Pour the custard back in and heat gently,
stirring constantly, for 2–3 minutes. The mixture should thicken
enough to coat the back of a wooden spoon in a thin layer.
Remove the pan from the heat.

NOTE

For convenience, make the custard up to 4 hours in advance.
If you are not serving the custard immediately, pour it into a jug.
Cover the surface with a circle of wet greaseproof paper to
prevent a skin from forming, then cover with clingfilm and chill.
To serve hot, reheat very gently.

Vanilla custard

Raspberry Coulis

Brandy Butter

RASPBERRY COULIS

To serve four to six, you will need:

225g (8oz) raspberries, 2 tbsp Kirsch or framboise eau de vie (optional), icing sugar to taste.

1 Put the raspberries into a blender or food processor with the Kirsch or eau de vie, if using. Whiz until they are completely puréed.
2 Transfer the purée to a fine sieve, then using a spoon, press and scrape it through the sieve until nothing is left but the pips.
3 Sweeten with icing sugar to taste and chill in the fridge until needed.

VARIATION

Use different soft fruits and liqueurs. For example, try crème de cassis with blackcurrants or Amaretto with apricots.

CHANTILLY CREAM

To serve eight, you will need:

284ml carton double cream, 1 tbsp golden caster sugar, finely grated zest of 1 orange (optional).

1 Whip the cream with the sugar until it forms soft peaks. Fold in half the grated orange zest, if you like. Cover and chill until needed.
2 Serve the Chantilly cream sprinkled with the remaining orange zest, if you like.

NOTE

Flavour the Chantilly cream with 2 tbsp Grand Marnier to serve with fruity puddings.

BRANDY BUTTER

To serve eight, you will need:

150g (5oz) unsalted butter, at room temperature, 150g (5oz) golden icing sugar, sifted, 3 tbsp brandy.

1 Put the butter into a bowl and whisk to soften. Gradually whisk in the icing sugar, pouring in the brandy just before the final addition. Continue whisking until the mixture is pale and fluffy, then spoon into a serving dish.
2 Cover and chill until needed. Remove from the fridge 30 minutes before serving.

NOTE

For a light, fluffy texture, whisk the brandy butter using an electric mixer just before serving.

CRÈME PÂTISSIÈRE

To make 450ml (¾ pint) you will need:

300ml (½ pint) full-fat milk, 1 vanilla pod, split, or 1 tsp vanilla extract, 3 medium egg yolks, beaten, 50g (2oz) golden caster sugar, 2 tbsp plain flour, 2 tbsp cornflour.

1 Pour the milk into a heavy-based pan. Scrape the vanilla seeds into the milk and add the pod, or add the vanilla extract. Slowly bring to the boil, take off the heat and leave to infuse for 10 minutes. Discard the pod.
2 Whisk the egg yolks and sugar together in a bowl until thick and creamy, then whisk in the flour and cornflour until smooth. Gradually whisk in the hot milk, then strain back into the pan. Slowly bring to the boil, whisking constantly. Cook, stirring, for 2–3 minutes until thickened and smooth. Pour into a bowl, cover the surface with a circle of wet greaseproof paper and leave to cool. Use as a filling for fruit flans and other pastries.

GLOSSARY

• •

All-in-one One of several basic methods for making cakes. Ingredients – usually sugar, eggs, flour and baking powder – are mixed together in a bowl, all in one go.

Almond paste A thick paste made from ground almonds, caster sugar and icing sugar. Often used to cover fruit cakes, it provides a flat surface for icing. Almond paste is also known as marzipan, although products labelled 'marzipan' tend to have a higher sugar content.

Baking blind Pre-baking a pastry case before filling. The pastry case is lined with greaseproof paper and weighted down with dried beans or ceramic baking beans.

Baking powder A raising agent consisting of an acid, usually cream of tartar and an alkali, such as bicarbonate of soda, which react to produce carbon dioxide. This expands during baking and makes cakes and breads rise.

Beat To incorporate air into an ingredient or mixture by agitating it vigorously with a spoon, fork, whisk or electric mixer. The technique is also used to soften ingredients.

Bind To mix beaten egg or other liquid into a dry mixture to hold it together.

Blanch To immerse food briefly in fast-boiling water to loosen skins, such as peaches, or to remove bitterness.

Buttercream A soft icing used to cover and fill cakes, made by creaming together butter and sugar.

Calorie Strictly a kilocalorie, this is used in dietetics to measure the energy value of foods.

Caramelise To heat sugar or sugar syrup slowly until it is brown in colour; that is, it forms a caramel.

Chill To cool food in the fridge.

Choux Soft, light pastry, either sweet or savoury, baked as profiteroles, eclairs or buns. It is very moist, creating steam when cooked and causing the pastry to puff up. It is usually filled with whipped cream after baking.

Combine To stir two or more ingredients together until mixed.

Compote Mixture of fresh or dried fruit stewed in sugar syrup. Served hot or cold.

Coulis A smooth fruit purée, thinned if necessary to a pouring consistency.

Consistency Term used to describe the texture of a mixture, for example, firm, dropping or soft.

Cream (ingredient) Made from the butterfat layer skimmed off the top of milk. Different types contain different percentages of butterfat, the higher the percentage, the easier the cream is to whip: **Single cream** (18% fat) has the thinnest consistency. It is not suitable for whipping and is used for pouring and in cooking. **Whipping cream** (at least 38% fat) can be whipped to twice its original volume. **Double cream** (48% fat) can be poured or whipped. **Extra thick cream** is single or double cream that has been homogenized to give it a thicker consistency, generally used only for spooning. **Clotted cream** (55% fat) does not need to be whipped and is generally not used during cooking as it separates when heated. **Soured cream** (18% fat) is single cream treated with a bacteria culture to give it a slightly sour taste and a thick texture. **Crème fraîche** (39% fat) is similar to soured cream, but slightly milder and softer. Creams with a fat content of 35% or above are suitable for freezing for up to 2 months.

Cream (technique) To beat together fat and sugar until the mixture is pale and fluffy and resembles whipped cream in texture and colour. The method is used in cakes and puddings that contain a high proportion of fat and require the incorporation of a lot of air.

Cream of tartar Also known as tartaric acid, this is a raising agent that is also an ingredient of baking powder and self-raising flour.

Crème pâtissière A rich egg custard that is often used to fill cakes and pastries, such as profiteroles and éclairs.

Crêpe French term for a pancake.

Crimp To decorate the edge of a pie, tart, shortbread or cake by pinching it at regular intervals to give a fluted effect. Special crimping tools are used to give a decorative edge to fondant-iced cakes.

Crystallise To preserve edible flowers or fruit in sugar.

Curdle To cause sauces or creamed mixtures to separate once the egg is added, usually by overheating or over-beating.

Dredge To sprinkle food generously with flour, sugar, icing sugar, and so on.

Dropping consistency Term used to describe the required texture of a cake or pudding mixture just before cooking. Test for it by taking a spoonful of the mixture and holding the spoon on its side above the bowl. The mixture should fall of its own accord within 5 seconds.

Dust To sprinkle lightly with flour, cornflour, icing sugar, and so on.

Extract Concentrated flavouring, which is used in small quantities; for example, vanilla extract.

Ferment Chemical change deliberately or accidentally brought about by fermenting agents, such as yeast or bacteria. Fermentation is utilised for making bread, yogurt, beer and wine.

Filo Delicate sheet pastry used to make fruit or savoury parcels, scrunched up as a topping on pies, and layered to create desserts such as baklava.

Flour Generally made from grinding wheat, this is the basis for breads, cakes and pasta, among other basic recipes. **White or plain flour** has had most of the wheat germ removed and is commonly used in cakes, in conjunction with a raising agent such as baking powder, as well as in biscuits, pastry and some breads. **Self-raising flour** is plain flour with a raising agent included. **Wholemeal flour** contains the whole of the wheatgerm, producing a denser result, which is higher in fibre. **Strong flour** is made from high-gluten wheat varieties, which helps dough to expand and rise. It is often used for bread-making. **Gluten-free flour** is usually made from a combination of ground rice, potato, buckwheat and maize.

Folding in Method of combining a whisked or creamed mixture with other ingredients by cutting and folding so that it retains its lightness. A large metal spoon or plastic-bladed spatula is used.

Fondant icing Pliable, all-purpose icing made from icing sugar, egg white and glucose, used to cover cakes and for modelling decorations. Also known as 'ready-to-roll icing'.

Frosting To coat leaves and flowers with a fine layer of sugar to use as a decoration. Also an American term for icing cakes.

Galette Cooked savoury or sweet mixture shaped into a round.

Ganache A rich filling or coating for cakes, choux buns and biscuits, made from chocolate and double cream.

Gelatine An animal-derived gelling agent, sold in powdered form and as leaf gelatine.

Gelazone A vegetarian gelling agent sold in powdered form in sachets, and used as a substitute for gelatine.

Glaze A glossy coating given to sweet and savoury dishes to improve their appearance and sometimes flavour. Ingredients for glazes include beaten egg, egg white, milk and syrup.

Gluten A protein constituent of grains, such as wheat and rye, which develops when the flour is mixed with water to give the dough elasticity.

Griddle A flat, heavy, metal plate used on the hob for cooking scones or for searing ingredients.

Grind To reduce foods such as nuts and whole spices to small particles using a food mill, pestle and mortar, electric grinder or food processor.

Hull To remove the stalk and calyx from soft fruits, such as strawberries.

Infuse To immerse flavourings, such as aromatic vegetables, herbs, spices and vanilla, in a liquid to impart flavour. Usually the infused liquid is brought to the boil, then left to stand for a while.

Knead To work dough by pummelling with the heel of the hand.

Knock back To knead yeast dough a second time after rising, to ensure an even texture.

Kugelhopf mould Tube-shaped, deep container with fluted sides, used for baking a traditional Austrian yeast cake of the same name.

Macerate To soften and flavour raw or dried foods by soaking in a liquid; for example, soaking fruit in alcohol.

Madeleine tray A baking tin with 12 shell-shaped indentations for baking traditional French madeleines.

Mandolin A flat wooden or metal frame with adjustable blades for slicing vegetables.

Mocha Term which has come to mean a blend of chocolate and coffee.

Muffin case Paper casing for cooking cupcakes and muffins.

Muffin tin Tray of cup-shaped moulds for cooking small cakes and deep tartlets. Also called a bun tin.

Parboil To boil a vegetable or other food for part of its cooking time before finishing it by another method.

Pare To finely peel the skin or zest from fruit.

Pâte The French word for pastry, familiar in pâte sucrée, a sweet flan pastry.

Patty tin Tray of cup-shaped moulds for cooking small cakes and deep tartlets. Also called a bun tin.

Pectin A naturally occurring substance found in most varieties of fruit and some vegetables, which is necessary for setting jams and jellies. Commercial pectin and sugar with pectin are also available for preserve-making.

Pestle and mortar Heavy marble or porcelain bowl with a heavy grinding tool for grinding herbs, spices, nuts, and so on.

Pith The bitter white skin under the thin zest of citrus fruit.

Pizza stone A clay stone for pizza baking, which reproduces the intense heat of a professional pizza oven.

Prove To leave bread dough to rise (usually for a second time) after shaping.

Puff A light, flaky pastry, made by repeatedly layering and rolling fat and pastry dough.

Purée To pound, sieve or liquidise fruit to a smooth pulp. Purées often form the basis for sauces.

Reduce To fast-boil stock or other liquid in an uncovered pan to evaporate water and concentrate the flavour.

Roulade Soufflé or sponge mixture rolled around a savoury or sweet filling.

Royal icing A traditional white icing made from sugar, lemon juice and egg whites, which dries to a hard finish. It is used for covering fruit cakes and also for piping decorations.

Rub-in Method of incorporating fat into flour by rubbing between the fingertips, used when a short texture is required. Used for pastry, cakes, scones and biscuits.

Run out Method of icing biscuits or cupcakes by piping a shape with royal icing and then 'flooding' it with thinned icing.

Shortcrust The simplest and quickest of the pastries to prepare at home, used for making tarts and pies. Sweet shortcrust pastry and rich shortcrust pastry can be made by adding sugar and egg yolk.

Sieve To press food through a perforated sieve to obtain a smooth texture.

Sift To shake dry ingredients through a sieve to remove lumps.

Simmer To keep a liquid just below boiling point.

Skim To remove froth or scum from the surface of jam, and so on. Use either a skimmer, a spoon or kitchen paper.

Spring-release tin Also known as a springform pan, this is a round cake tin with a spring-release side and removable base, which is clamped in. Used for cakes and desserts that are not to be inverted.

Steam To cook food in steam, usually in a steamer over rapidly boiling water.

Steep To immerse food in warm or cold liquid to soften it, and sometimes to draw out strong flavours.

Suet Hard fat of animal origin used in pastry and steamed puddings. A vegetarian alternative is readily available.

Sugar syrup A concentrated solution of sugar in water used to poach fruit and make sorbets, granitas, fruit juices.

Swiss roll tin Shallow, rectangular tin, available in several different sizes, used for baking sponges that are filled and rolled after baking – such as roulades.

Torte Rich cake made with little or no flour.

Tepid The term used to describe temperature at approximately blood heat: 37°C (98.7°F).

Thermometer, Sugar/Fat Used for accurately checking the temperature of boiling sugar syrups.

Unleavened Flat bread, such as pitta, made without a raising agent.

Vanilla sugar Sugar in which a vanilla pod has been stored to impart its flavour.

Whipping (whisking) Beating air rapidly into a mixture with a manual or electric whisk. Whipping usually refers to cream. Whisking can also refer to the basic cake-making technique, in which the sugar and eggs are whisked together over a pan of simmering water. Melted butter and flour are then folded into the mixture.

Zest The thin coloured outer layer of citrus fruit, which can be removed in fine strips with a zester.

INDEX

PICTURE CREDITS

• •